keep
love
alive

keep love *alive*

Linda Sonntag

HAMLYN

PHOTOGRAPHIC ACKNOWLEDGMENTS

The publishers wish to thank the following organizations and individuals for their kind permission to reproduce the photographs in this book:

Bubbles Photo Library: L. J. Thurston 34, 123 / Frans Rombout 111; Camera Press (U.K.) Ltd: Anna 120 / Jane Hilton 10, 60, 83 / Eliot Siegel 85; Collections: Anthea Sieveking 37, 99; Lupe Cunha: 51; Explorer: Jacques Joffre 25 bottom / Jean-Paul Nacivet 15 / Sarah Ney 97; Robert Harding Picture Library: 129; The Hutchison Library: K. Rodgers 24 bottom; The Image Bank: Werner Bokelberg 31, 38, 39, 113, 117 / S. Corrodi 107 / Schmid Langsfeld 65; Magnum Photos Ltd: Abbas 24 top / Leonard Freed 25 top; PWA International Ltd: 17; Reed International Books Ltd: Anthony Horth 6-7, 9, 12-13, 28-29, 43, 48-49, 69, 79, 88, 90-91, 114-115, 132-143; Tony Stone Worldwide: Andy Cox 93, 103 / Chris Craymer 73; Derek Russell-Stoneham: 21; Syndication International: 54, 57, 62-63, 67, 76-77; Transworld Features: 46; Zefa Picture Library (U.K.) Ltd: 125, 127.

First published in Great Britain 1993 by Hamlyn, an imprint of Reed Consumer Books Ltd., Michelin House, 81 Fulham Road, London SW3 6RB
and
Auckland, Melbourne, Singapore, and Toronto

Copyright 1993 © Reed International Books Limited

All rights reserved. No part of this publication may be reproduced, stored in a retrieval system, or transmitted, in any form or by any means, electronic, mechanical, photocopying, recording or otherwise, without the permission of the publisher and copyright holder.

ISBN 0 600 57646 9

Printed in Hong Kong

CONTENTS

INTRODUCTION

PARTNERSHIPS
WHAT IS THIS THING CALLED LOVE? 8
THE NEED TO SHARE 14
LOVE AND COMMITMENT 20

TOGETHERNESS
DEPENDENCE AND INDEPENDENCE 30
UNDERSTANDING YOUR PARTNER 36
INTIMACY AND SEXUAL FULFILMENT 42
SOLVING SEXUAL PROBLEMS 50
CONFLICT 64
INFIDELITY 72
JEALOUSY 84

FAMILY LIFE
FROM COUPLE TO FAMILY 92
PREGNANCY AND CHILDBIRTH 96
A BABY IN THE HOUSE 102
CHILDREN AND YOUR RELATIONSHIP 106
THE GROWING FAMILY 110

STAYING IN TOUCH
KEEPING YOUR RELATIONSHIP ALIVE 116
UNDERSTANDING STRESS 122
RELAXATION TECHNIQUES 128

introduction

Choosing a partner, to marry or to live with in a long-term relationship, is the most important personal decision that anyone can ever make. And then what? Is there such a thing as happily ever after? It's at the point of commitment that fairy tales end; and that's where this book begins.

The divorce rate may be rising, but statistics show that most couples still manage to stay together. Is staying together enough? Does the feeling of being in love have to wear off? Does choosing commitment mean saying yes to comfort and goodbye to passion?

In the early days of a relationship when everything is new and fresh, partners talk and listen in order to discover one another. They tune into each other with all their senses. But familiarity breeds laziness; it numbs the senses.

The passing of time and increased responsibilities – such as having children – bring more routine and make it difficult not to conform to a role. As you fulfill the requirements for being a wife, husband or parent, do you ask yourself where your individuality has disappeared to? Do you sometimes wonder who this person is, with whom you share your life?

Keep Love Alive aims to help you answer these questions. It attempts to explore ways in which you can keep your relationship alive and growing, by staying in touch with your own and your partner's feelings; by being yourself, and not letting your role take over; and by remaining vulnerable and affirming your interest and attraction.

Being in a long-term relationship gives you unlimited time and a base of security: the scope you need for exploring who you both are. The quest for knowledge can continue all your life: the secret is to retain your curiosity.

Note

This book is written for both women and men, and unless specific mention is made, the advice in it applies to both sexes. However, since repeating 'he or she' throughout would be cumbersome, the text is addressed mainly to the female reader.

partnerships

What is this thing called love?

Falling in love is the most exquisitely personal of all human experiences. When you fall in love all your senses come alive, making you uniquely aware of the world and of your own emotions.

When you fall in love, you radiate tremendous good will and discover a breadth of generosity, and a depth of understanding and compassion you did not know were possible. Love like this is a rare and precious phenomenon, and the urge to hold on to it is strong. It can force us into actions that change the rest of our lives. Yet being in love is an elusive experience: it seems to thrive on absence and uncertainty. In time, and with commitment, the splendour tends to fade.

So what exactly, after the initial excitement is over and the relationship has settled, does married love, committed love, consist of?

TYPES OF LOVE

Being in love with someone feels different to loving them, yet we have only the one word, 'love', to describe both emotional states. The Greeks recognized that there were two sorts of love, *eros* and *agape*. Eros, of course, was passion, whereas agape was deep and enduring love, the love of commitment.

● EROS This is an all-consuming love: it absorbs all of the attention and colours every aspect of life. Erotic love is dynamic: fraught with mystery and drama. Eros is particularly strong when the love relationship is in its early precarious stages. It involves yearning and longing when the beloved person is not there, and rapture and excitement shot through with doubt and anxiety when the lovers are together.

Sexual attraction is the strongest characterisic of this sort of love, and this is usually heightened by obstacles put in the way of its fulfilment. The original meaning of 'passion' is 'suffering': the lovers are prepared to endure pain and hardship for each other's sake, and the extent of their suffering is seen as an indication of the depth of their love.

What is this thing called love?

Partnerships

● AGAPE This is love without tension: it is calm and not frantic. It encompasses security and understanding; it is a love that sustains with support and comfort. It thrives in an atmosphere of mutual trust and respect, and allows freedom and individual development. This is a mature love that runs through an established relationship like a mighty underground river. Ever-present but not intrusive or overwhelming, it provides a base from which both partners can pursue their own goals in the world, and to which they can return to share their experiences. Serenity is its keynote. Energy is not consumed but recharged, to be focused outwards into the world. Partners in agape cherish each other, nurturing the positive aspects of their relationship and tolerating its failings.

Eros strikes out of the blue; it is the subject of every love story. Agape is the 'happily ever after' love, and much more difficult to achieve. Both types of love have their glories, and both have potentially negative aspects. Love affairs are remarkable for the acute intensity of the feelings that carry them forward, but the tumultuousness of eros can be destructive: it can drive people insane, break their hearts and cause them to hate and even kill. The pitfalls of committed love are of a different order, because a relationship lacking in tension and excitement is liable to degenerate into apathy and boredom.

IS THERE EXCITEMENT AFTER COMMITMENT?

When two people enter a commitment, they are making a pledge to each other to banish uncertainty and insecurity from their relationship. But instability fuels passion, so how can a stable relationship remain passionate?

Passion is gradually extinguished by familiarity, habit and routine. The structure of your relationship can begin to obscure the individuals within it. It's only too easy to lose sight of your partner as a person once you have got used to them playing a certain role in your life (breadwinner, child-rearer, the one who cooks, the one who deals with the financial aspects of domestic life, etc.). And it's impossible to feel passion for someone you take for granted. When the urgency has gone from your relationship and your interest has slackened, it's still easy to assume that you are close to your partner because that is the person you observe in action every day. However, you can be constantly in someone's company without knowing anything about the reality of their inner life, or having the first idea of their most private thoughts and feelings.

A VOYAGE OF DISCOVERY

The way to keep love alive in a committed relationship is to replace the excitement of insecurity and longing with the more profound thrill of a journey of discovery. As life unfolds, you and your partner change and grow in different ways. Be aware of your own development, and stay in tune with your partner's thoughts and emotions. Talk about the way you see yourselves and each other, and plumb your deepest fears and longings. Get close: ask, tell. Take the risk of discovering less than comfortable feelings in your quest for knowledge. So many couples jog along in predictable and companionable routines because it is too difficult – or frightening – to explore the depths of their personalities. They picture themselves as contentedly 'side by side'. This is a perfectly adequate arrangement for offering comfort and support, but it ignores intimacy, the whole world of riches that commitment has to offer.

Emotional intimacy requires active engagement and cannot be achieved by partners who run on parallel lines. True knowledge of your partner – partly through developing intuition and aware-

Partnerships

ness, partly through asking and telling – is the most exciting and fulfilling of the riches that committed love has to offer. In the Bible, the verb 'to know' is used to signify sexual love, and intimate knowledge of another person is deeply erotic. To truly know someone is to penetrate their personality; to accept what you find there, good and not so good, is to love that person. To allow someone to penetrate your own personality is to be open and vulnerable to them, to trust them with the parts of yourself you find difficult to fathom and to give yourself in

What is this thing called love?

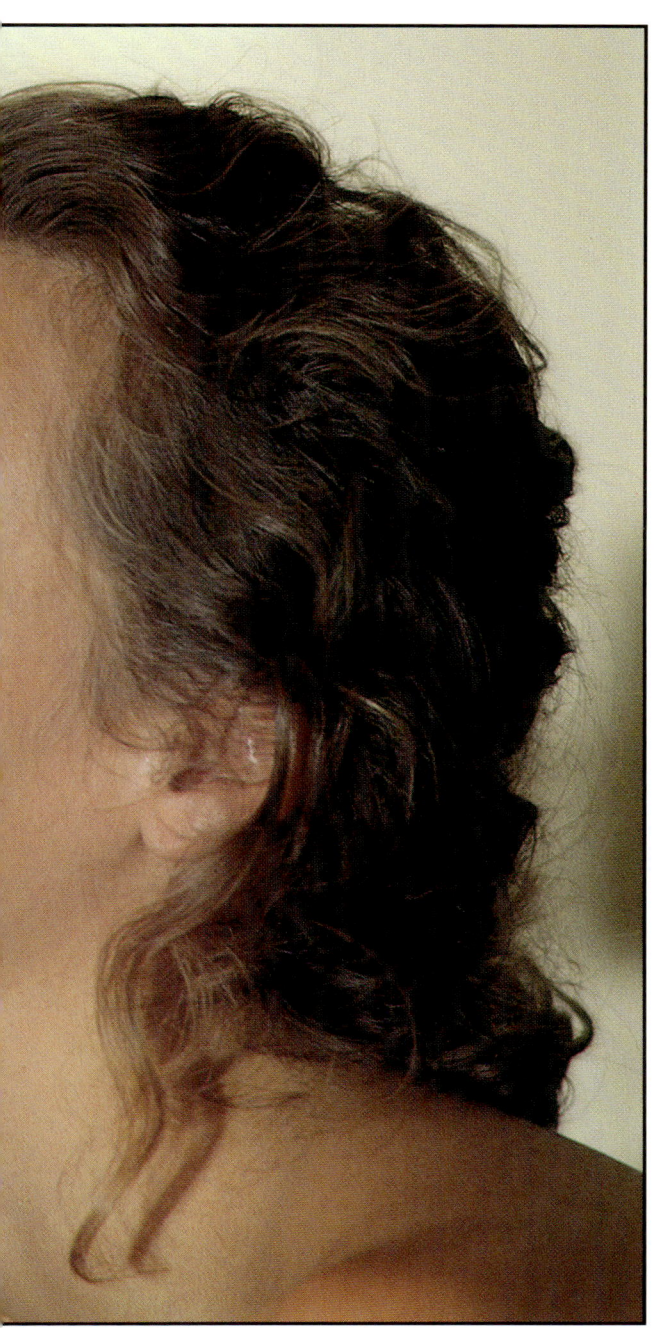

ing this in a lecture, the novelist said that although we think we fall in love because of sexual attraction, what we are really looking for is someone who is 'able to hear us'. Elsewhere there is a true story of a man who sat for a woman painter. Day after day she studied him intently, transferring what she learned about him through her eyes to the canvas. The man was deeply moved by being looked at so minutely, so searchingly, and when he saw the portrait he was amazed by the perceptiveness of her interpretation of his character. During the sittings he had fallen in love with the painter, and now, overwhelmed, he took her in his arms.

These two stories show that the key ingredient in deep erotic love is knowledge achieved by listening and looking, by paying close attention. This kind of knowledge is an ongoing process of active participation and deepens with the years. The couple who sit side by side, who are used to each other and listen with only half an ear because they've heard it all before, pay for comfort with boredom. In their relationship, the dynamics of erotic love have lapsed. They may still have sex, but there won't be any passion in it. However, the couple who interact, who pay attention, who really listen and really look at one another, kindle deep erotic love through layer upon layer of creative understanding and acceptance. The excitement of erotic love need never fade from your relationship as long as you develop ears to hear each other and eyes to see.

love. This two-way process is renewed every time your conversation with your partner breaks new ground.

In her novel *The Temple of My Familiar*, Alice Walker has one of her characters fall in love with a man because she sees him as 'a giant ear'. In explain-

the need to share

When he wrote the now famous words 'No man is an Island', the poet John Donne was recognizing that we all need to make connections with each other in order to realize our humanity.

We connect with the other adults we meet in our daily lives on different levels in an ascending scale of personal involvement. The more personal involvement there is, the more fulfilling a relationship is likely to be, but we need to exercise ourselves on all levels of involvement in order to take our place in the community and in society at large.

At the bottom of the scale there is virtually no scope for exercising individuality: in dealing with officials we are hampered by bureaucratic rules and regulations that render people anonymous. Higher up the scale come business and commercial transactions, which can sometimes allow for a dash of personality; then come relations with colleagues at work, and with other people with whom we deal on a friendly but professional basis, such as shopkeepers, the doctor, the plumber etc. These all benefit from a certain degree of personal warmth. Then come the people with whom our relationships are wholly personal: on the first tier, our aquaintances and neighbours, to whom we hope to show good will, or at least politeness; on the second, friends and family with whom we enjoy spending leisure time; on the third, our closest friends in whom we can confide; and finally, our partner, our mate, our 'other half'.

This closest and most personal of relationships has the potential to be the most rewarding of all, but it can also be the most problematical. The vast majority of people (90 per cent) commit themselves to sharing their lives with a mate at some stage, in the hope that the union will be long-term, if not permanent. But most adults spend some time living alone either before or after long-term relationships, and some prefer the single life.

Whether single or coupled, our relationships form a large part of our lives. Yet our basic education provides us with little insight into how to handle them.

The need to share

Learning to relate

Psychologists believe that our first close relationship – that with our mother – provides a model on which we build our intimate relationships as adults. Martin Richards of Cambridge University has analysed videos of mothers and babies and shown that their head movements and eye contacts in interaction with each other form a kind of dance – a closely linked pattern of action and response. In addition, mothers talk to their babies as if they could already reason and make decisions: it's a way of forming the structure of a relationship in which the child can grow to take its own part.

Autistic children cannot respond to their mother's voice and eye contact, and grow up locked in a world of their own without the ability to relate. It has also been shown that normal children who have been deprived of attention and affection experience great difficulties forming relationships as adults.

It is possible that in our relationships with our partners we are seeking something of the original exclusive bond that we enjoyed with our mothers. We look for the kind of caring we first knew. Of course what is familiar to us is not always what is best for us: someone who experienced an element of neglect in their first relationship can often subconsciously choose partners who also behave neglectfully. And someone who had a mother who lavished attention and care on them without really being aware of, or meeting, their real individual needs, may choose partners who seem loving but leave them feeling oddly unfulfilled.

At times, we all need our partners to provide the detailed in-depth caring, the one-hundred-per-cent attention that a loving mother focuses on her baby. But unlike babies, as adults we find if difficult to tolerate unlimited attention without feeling smothered.

What a partner can provide

Relating to other people is an important way of getting to know yourself and of developing into the person you want to be. Bouncing your ideas and opinions off others is a way of defining them: seeing them through the eyes of others may reveal ways in which they need to be modified in order for you to own them more fully. Learning other people's ideas and their reasons for having them is to broaden your outlook and develop tolerance and respect; the more you respect others, the more you forgive yourself your own defects, and the more deserving you become of respect yourself. Learning to care for others, to give and to receive, opens the way for others to care for and respect you.

The process of building relationships is cyclical and self-enriching, and the higher up the relationship is on the scale of personal involvement, the more mutually satisfying it is likely to be. At the top of the scale, your partner should be the person who knows you best, and before whom you can reveal yourself most fully. In front of your partner, as with no one else, you should be able to relax and simply be yourself, in the secure knowledge

The need to share

that you are completely accepted. He or she is the person above all others who shares your beliefs, your tastes and your sense of humour, who appreciates your personality, and who understands you. Over the years, your partner builds up a unique and irreplaceable bank of knowledge about you, and this becomes your true home base. Sharing understanding with your partner should give you the secure feeling of touching base.

Your partner should be a person who likes you and is interested in you, and therefore pays close attention to you. Attention is a matter of listening, asking and confirming understanding. Through your partner's attention you are affirmed in your personality and you acquire the self-esteem that equips you to deal with the rest of the world. Your interaction with your partner should give you new insights that strengthen your self-knowledge, and provide confirmation that you are a worthwhile person.

The dialogue between partners builds people. It is an active process, and without it your relationship will just tread water, or sink, and your personality will stagnate. The potential for mutual discovery and self-development is a rich seam running through every long-term relationship. It holds both sustenance and excitement, the ingredients for committed and erotic love. Curiously few people list it as one of their reasons for getting married.

THE SINGLE LIFE

The advantages of being single are especially attractive for people who have developed strongly individual tastes and idiosyncratic lifestyles. Such independent people are not suited to the slowing of pace and the loss of privacy that come with sharing domestic arrangements, nor do they adapt well to compromise, which is essential in many practical aspects of living together.

Many independent people are strongly territorial, and could not accommodate the 'invasion' of their home, their cupboard space and book shelves by another person, however dearly loved. By forfeiting domestic companionship, which to them may seem claustrophobic, single people do not need to forgo the benefits of intimacy. Often the most successful arrangement for the independent type is to have a lover who is equally committed to the single life; and single people tend to develop particularly strong bonds with a handful of close friends.

The ideal single life is perhaps a combination of time spent alone to allow for solitary pursuits; time spent with a lover, to provide intensity; and time spent with close friends, to provide a sense of continuity and permanence.

The need to share

WHY MEN AND WOMEN SAY THEY MARRY

In her wide ranging questionnaires the eminent American sexologist Shere Hite has asked thousands of women and men why they married. The answers of both sexes were surprisingly similar:

WOMEN SAID THEY MARRIED
- *For companionship, a sense of belonging, stability*
- *To build a shared past and plan a shared future*
- *Because they liked caring for somebody, feeling needed, sharing pleasure*
- *Because they enjoyed feeling that they were number one in their partners' lives*
- *Because marriage was a haven*
- *Because it meant they would not have to face life alone*
- *For warmth and closeness*
- *In order to have children (although most women without children preferred being childless, and half of the women with children regretted the loss to their careers)*

MEN SAID THEY MARRIED
- *For domestic warmth*
- *For security, and the stability and regularity of home life*
- *Because they wanted someone to help them and care for them*

An important additional reason that prompted some men to marry was the fact that their wives performed services round the home that made married life more comfortable for them than living alone (see Housework, page 33).

Surprisingly, only a handful of men and an equally small number of women mentioned sex as a reason for marrying. Another surprise was that few mentioned their love or liking for their specific partner, or the possibility of personal development or growth through their relationship. Only 13 per cent of women said that they were still in love with their husbands after two years.

It could be that these factors are connected: that people fall out of love with their partners and that sex between them ceases to be exciting (or even worth mentioning in a survey), because they lose sight of each other as individuals and neglect to focus on opportunities for growth and development. The women and men questioned by Shere Hite have a vision of marriage that is secure, comfortable, companionable and cosy: static rather than dynamic. It's the set-up that appeals to most married people rather than the person they are with. He or she becomes part of the domestic furniture, recreating the familiar atmosphere of the original home in which they grew up. What is lacking is the feeling of acute personal involvement. And it is this alone that creates the climate of deepening knowledge and intimacy in which powerful sex can thrive.

love and commitment

Real emotional commitment grows naturally out of love. It does not happen by choice or design. No one can be persuaded or forced into it, and once there, its existence cannot be denied.

Commitment is a feeling rather than a contractual agreement, and it builds up over time, gradually.

You will know you are committed when the realization dawns that your partner is your irreplaceable best friend, a person with whom you are fascinated and for whom you are prepared to do your utmost. If this relationship takes priority above all others, you will willingly help each other practically and emotionally in any way you can, and you will look forward to staying together through changing circumstances and to making long-term plans.

Because commitment is knowledge and acceptance of the whole person, couples who are secure in each other are free to be more open about their opinions than they were when they first met, and this often means more arguments. If a couple pledge commitment but still feel insecure, their relationship is often dominated by the fear of the loss of the other person, and a lack of trust breeds suspicion and guilt.

WHAT DIFFERENCE DOES MARRIAGE MAKE?

Over 90 per cent of us marry at least once, making a public statement of our private commitment. To marry is to formalize an oath of stability and fidelity: to promise not to leave your partner when problems occur, and not to get involved sexually or romantically with anyone else.

Often people get married because their parents and society at large expect them to. It is 'the thing to do': friends and peers are getting married, and there is the feeling that not getting married is 'missing out' – on a big day when you and your partner are the centre of attention, on a big celebration for family and

Love and commitment

friends, on presents and a honeymoon; and missing out above all on a change of status that many still feel is important.

There is no doubt that the change of status is a very real one for couples who do not live together before marriage; from living alone or with friends or relatives to sharing a home and a new way of life with a partner is an enormous step and takes some adjusting to. Engaged couples will probably have been sexually faithful to each other for a good while, so loss of sexual freedom on marrying will not affect them, but losing other forms of freedom may not be so easy. Suddenly, privacy and independence disappear: time and what happens in it is no longer in your control, and decision making becomes a shared process.

On the plus side, couples hope to gain security, closeness and sexual fulfilment, and a permanent social partner. However, these things cannot be achieved instantly, and the early days of sharing married life in a new home can be a disappointment and a let-down after all the hullaballoo of the wedding.

Increasingly, many couples live together before marriage. Many just naturally move towards sharing. They may spend weekends together, leave clothes and belongings in each other's homes, and gradually find their households merging, until one home seems redundant, and a waste of money to keep on. So they move in together. They already know what to expect of each other, and that their lifestyles mesh in a satisfactory way, so they have none of the fears or unrealistic expectations of newlyweds moving into their first home.

Some couples who live together never feel the need to marry, but others do. They may simply marry to celebrate the success of their relationship. Or they may marry because they have decided to start a family, and feel that making a public commitment will give their children a more stable home. But inevitably, some couples marry because their relationship is already going drastically wrong, and they hope that marriage will glue it back together again and give it a new lease of life. Needless to say, marriage as a salvage operation rarely works.

Couples who have been living together happily before marriage may notice no difference at all once they have tied the knot; but often there is a subtle shift of emphasis that is purely psychological, but no less real for that. For some the experience is beneficial, and they report increased feelings of relaxation and security. But others complain of an annoying sense of having 'given in to convention', and a loss of independence and integrity that they bitterly regret.

It is mainly women who feel that their status has been diminished by marriage, and that instead of being equals with their partners, they are now expected to take the subservient role. A study conducted in the United States would seem to bear this out, because whereas only one in 10 single men wanted their partners to give up work, one in three married men would prefer their wives to stay at home and be dependent on them.

The decision to marry is a very personal one. Before making it, you will need to think long and hard, both alone and in discussion together, about the psychological as well as the practical effects it will have on your lives. Try not to let yourselves be influenced by what your friends do, or by what your family and the community expect of you. Above all, realize that there are many ways of showing love and commitment to your partner. There is not just one right way to do it, and your way may well be different from the next couple's.

THE ENGAGEMENT

The idea of engagement originated in the sixth century, when the English King Ethelbert made it illegal for a man simply to canter up on his horse and remove the woman of his choice from her home by force. King Ethelbert was not thinking of the woman, however, but of the loss to her father of a useful pair of hands. Any man who 'stole' a woman was obliged to pay her 'owner' 50 shillings compensation for all the spinning she would have done; the unclaimed daughters of the house remained 'spinsters'.

The 'bride price' or 'wed', as it was called, sealed an agreement between the groom and the father of the bride, or sometimes between the fathers of both parties, that a marriage would take place.

Giving an engagement ring is a more recent custom and dates from Victorian times. The ring is the token of the pledge the couple make and, sparkling on the finger of the bride-to-be, it announces to other would-be suitors that her affections are already engaged.

The custom of placing the ring on the third finger of the left hand is an ancient one. The Romans believed that this finger contained the 'vein of love', which ran directly to the heart. A diamond is the most usual choice of stone for an engagement ring. This is partly because it is so hardwearing, but it also stems from a belief prevalent in Italy during the Middle Ages that it was the stone of reconciliation, capable of restoring harmony after a quarrel.

In recent years, the British royal family have popularized coloured stones for engagements, or the bride may choose her birthstone, or another gemstone whose symbolic meaning especially appeals to her.

MARRIAGE VERSUS LIVING TOGETHER: SOME PRACTICAL CONSIDERATIONS

Living together without marriage is now a widely accepted social phenomenon, and many couples do not bother to formalize their union, feeling that it is a private arrangement that does not need regulation by Church or State. For the purposes of this book, it is irrelevant whether a couple are married or not; however, some practical considerations, such as legal responsiblities and financial rights, are affected by marital status. Although they may make little difference to your lives at present, if no agreement has been drawn up they may cause trouble if you should decide to part.

Wedding Customs and Traditions

● The idea of having bridesmaids, pages, a best man and ushers originated with the belief that evil spirits, envious of the couple's happiness, would be out to harm them, but would be confused by so many similarly dressed people. The custom of the best man probably goes back to the days when the groom took a friend with him when he went to kidnap the bride from her home. Bells were originally rung at weddings to frighten away the evil spirits, and noisy celebrations were held beforehand to try and drive them from the community. These were the ancestors of our stag and hen parties.

● The Ancient Egyptians were probably the first to use wedding rings: in hieroglyphics, the circle was the symbol of eternity. The ring can also symbolize the bonds of a captive. In the 18th and 19th centuries it was not unknown for church officials to pay for the bride's ring as an inducement to marry.

● The Hindu ceremony takes place under a canopy of brocade or some other richly decorated material, festooned with flowers. The bride, wearing a red silk sari, is the first to arrive, but she hides out of sight until the bridegroom, robed in white, has been brought in by his friends and relations. As he enters, lights are waved over his head and grains of rice are

thrown, a ceremonial act symbolizing riches and fertility.

● In the Buddhist ceremony the bride and groom sip three times from each of three bowls of increasing size to symbolize how their lives will grow together.

● In past times it was customary to shower the bride and groom with petals as they left the church, and for them to walk along a path strewn with flowers. This charming idea gave way in the era of mass production to paper confetti. In some countries, rice is thrown, to symbolize fertility and plenty. Beware, it could hurt if thrown with great vigour!

● White wedding dresses have been in the forefront of bridal fashion since Queen Victoria broke with the royal tradition of a silver dress and opted for white for her wedding to Prince Albert in 1840.

● The going-away car is often decorated by high-spirited friends with messages in lipstick and shaving foam, and tied about with balloons, tin cans, and old boots. The 'old boot' tradition is an ancient one and stems from the time when the father, on giving away his daughter to the groom, presented him also with one of her slippers. This gave the new husband, symbolically speaking, the upper hand, for he was supposed to thrash her with it should she displease him. The slipper was put at the bed head on his side of the bed to remind his wife who was boss. However, if she became the dominant partner, neighbours transferred the power of the slipper to her, and christened her 'the old boot'.

● In the Jewish wedding ceremony the couple are married under a chuppah, a canopy of silk or velvet held up by four posts. This is a relic of the time when the children of Israel lived in tents. It symbolizes the bridal chamber. To some it signifies the home the couple will make together; its fragility reminds the couple of their own weakness and the need to nurture

their union in order to ensure its survival. During the ceremony the bride and groom drink wine from the same glass, symbolizing that they will share all things. The bridegroom then dashes the glass to the floor and grinds it under his foot. Some say that this is a reminder of the destruction of the Temple of Jerusalem, others that it frightens off the evil spirits; friends call out muzel tov ('good luck') at this point.

> ## WHAT THE LAW SAYS
>
> - *Under English law, a newlywed couple promise to look after one another, to live together, and to consent to sex, although this last promise has recently come increasingly under question, and it is now recognized legally that it is possible for a husband to rape his wife.*
>
> - *Married people cannot be called to give evidence against one another in court.*
>
> - *The law does not stipulate that a woman should take her husband's name on marrying him. It is legal to call yourself by any name that you choose, except of course for fraudulent purposes. Many married women now choose to retain their names, or to use their own name followed by their husband's, with a hyphen or without, as is the practice in America.*

MARRIAGE AND YOUR FINANCES

However optimistic you are about the future together, it is always a sensible idea to be perfectly clear as to who owns what. This is especially important if you are not married and about to become dependent on your partner's income, perhaps because you are pregnant and will give up work to look after the baby.

Married people who split up will probably be granted equal shares of the value of their home, even if only the prime wage-earner's name is on the deeds. In addition, the wife may be granted maintenance, whether or not she has any children by the union.

For unmarried people the story is a very different one. Even though they may have been just as established a partnership as if they were married, under law they are regarded as two separate individuals, and the law stipulates that property should go to whichever one is its rightful owner. It is a messy and expensive business trying to contest ownership, so the golden rules are:

- *Make sure that both your names are on the title deeds to your home.*

- *Always keep proof of ownership of major items, or draw up and sign an agreement of ownership or joint ownership. Consult a solicitor for advice.*

Both these rules are extremely important, not only for your self-protection, but also for the protection of your heirs, should you die (see opposite).

As far as income tax is concerned, there is little difference in the way married and unmarried couples are taxed (married couples are now also treated as individuals; formerly a wife's earnings were seen purely as an adjunct to her husband's income, and she was not even allowed to fill in her own tax form). However, a slight advantage remains to married couples. In addition to their personal tax allowance, they are also granted a married couple's allowance, although in real terms this is decreasing as the years go by. Certain tax exemptions may also benefit the married couple where transfers or gifts of large amounts of money are concerned. By contrast, unmarried couples who transfer assets to each other are liable for Capital Gains Tax and Inheritance Tax.

When drawing social security benefits, no differentiation is made between couples who are married and those who are not. All people who are living with others get a lower rate of benefit than people living alone.

If your partner (married or not) runs up debts on a joint account or credit card, or leaves you with an enormous phone bill, you will be liable. However, any personal debts are that person's sole responsibility.

Marriage and your children

In legal disputes over children, the law always puts the welfare of the children first, whether you are married or not. But unmarried partners have fewer legal rights where their children are concerned. The father may not even be registered on the child's birth certificate, although this can be arranged. The mother has the right to decide in important matters such as her children's schooling, welfare and religion. If unmarried parents split up, the father is not automatically given rights of contact with his children. If he wants contact and his partner will not allow it, he will have to get a court order granting it. An unmarried mother will not be granted maintenance, although a married mother can get maintenance through a court order if it is not willingly given.

The importance of making a will

If you die intestate (without having made a will), your estate will be divided according to intestacy laws. Much of it could be lost to the state, and the person or people whom you would wish to benefit may end up with nothing at all. It is particularly important to draw up a will if you are living in a committed but unmarried relationship, which the laws of intestacy do not acknowledge.

● *An unmarried person does not have automatic rights to the estate of their deceased partner, and relatives would have a prior claim. If the deceased was still married but living in a new relationship, the estranged spouse could benefit, causing much suffering to the new partner.*

● *An unmarried person has no automatic rights to a deceased partner's company or private pension payments, and nor can a deceased partner's national insurance contributions be taken into account when assessing a woman's entitlement to state retirement pension if she has not paid enough contributions herself. Make sure you are named as beneficiary on each other's pension funds.*

togetherness

dependence and independence

One of the major sacrifices you make in forming a couple is giving up your independence. This is particularly true for women, who put themselves second in the eyes of society when they pair up with a man.

Since the '60s, feminism has made great strides in putting the balance right, but one consequence of feminist effort is that women today sometimes find themselves feeling guilty if they don't want to be independent working wives and mothers.

Love does peculiar things to us, and love for a good man may awaken in the most committedly independent woman a deep longing to be cared for. This is nothing to feel ashamed of. The whole point of the Women's Liberation movement was to ensure that women had the power to choose and the confidence to use that power. If your choice is to stay at home and look after the house and your children while your husband works, then that choice is every bit as valid as the choice of another woman who devotes herself to her career, or the choice of another who combines a career and children and has to employ a childminder.

Whatever share of responsibility you each take for providing the income and the labour needed to maintain your home, the vital thing is to make the choice that is right for you. And however much you care for your home and your partner, don't forget that everyone needs the occasional break from homemaking, career-building and raising children to develop their own personal interests.

SHARING FINANCIAL RESPONSIBILITY

If you choose to give up work, you will of course be dependent on your partner's income, but that does not make you the dependant and him the provider in every area of your life together. Dependence and independence are also states of mind; they are not fixed, and fluctuate according to how strong you both feel.

Dependence and independence

He may support you financially, but this should not stop you being emotionally interdependent. When one feels down, the other can give comfort and encouragement, and vice versa. There is no such thing as being equal all the time.

According to one survey, 70 per cent of women now go out to work, and there is no doubt that their contribution in the workplace constitutes an important part of their realization of equality and self-worth. Most of the women who took part in American sexologist Shere Hite's questionnaires found financial dependence demeaning – one woman described her life staying at home as being no more than that of a 'housekeeper, cook, prostitute and nurse'.

Most women go out to work, partly for economic reasons and partly also because they enjoy having a life of their own outside the home. Earning money, no matter how little, means power and choice. It means not watching the man of the house depart in the morning in a smart suit while you're wearing your oldest clothes in readiness for polishing the floor. It means having friends and colleagues of your own. It means having problems and challenges to solve that are more interesting than those discovered when hoovering the carpet or ordering the coal. It means having your own bank account, your own money with which you can buy clothes without feeling guilty.

Of course there are also plenty of women in top jobs who earn as much as their husbands, if not more, and for these there is career satisfaction plus the knowledge that they contribute at least half of the family income. However, high-earning women may have a problem if their husbands feel diminished by earning less than they do. A lot of men still feel threatened by a woman who can command a good salary: a throwback to the days when men relied on their sole power as wage-earners to give them superior status.

It is interesting to note that whichever partner earns more, it is the woman who tends to be in charge of the household's financial arrangements (just as she is almost invariably in charge of the housework, see opposite). When couples first start to live together, they are often at a loss as to how to divide financial responsibility. There are three basic alternatives to consider:

1. *Each partner pays for certain items each month. Perhaps he pays the mortgage, while she pays for gas, electricity and telephone. He might also pay for the car and their holidays, while she pays the grocery bills. He might buy the drink, while she buys the children's clothes. This system is usually worked out so that each spends the same proportion of their earnings on running the household, and both have spending money left over. This is a good system because it doesn't penalize the one who earns less.*

2. *The earnings of both are pooled in a joint account. All bills are paid out of this account. In theory this is the least complicated system, but in practice it can*

often cause conflict, especially if one partner is in the habit of making purchases that the other thinks are extravagant and unnecessary.

3. *All bills, from the mortgage to a small purchase at the corner shop, are split equally down the middle. This is a strictly fair system, but it is time-consuming and it can seem nitpicking. A major disadvantage is that it can leave the one who earns less with little or no spending money.*

HOUSEWORK

Housework is a thorny issue in many homes. It used to be considered women's work, and there are still women who choose to be housewives and willingly take sole responsibility for cooking, washing up, tidying up, cleaning, laundry, ironing and bed making, usually in addition to looking after the children. If that is their choice, fine. But many more women find themselves shouldering all or most of the burden of household responsibilities against their will.

This is particularly true of women who, faced with the option of having a career or having a family, decide on both. These women can find themselves in an interminable round of delivering and collecting their children at both ends of a demanding day's work, with an evening of domestic chores afterwards. There is no time for relaxing with their partners, or in which they can develop their own interests, and at the end of an exhausting day they are not likely to have any energy left over for lovemaking.

If working mothers complain that there's never any time, their partners may say, considerately: 'If it's too much for you doing a job on top of all the rest of it, you can always give up your job. We should be able to manage on my salary alone'. To spend her entire life trapped in the domestic round may seem an unappealing alternative for the overworked mother whose job gives her a valued feeling of freedom and independence, but is it the only solution? It is surely ironic that in this age of equality, it is still only women who are expected to decide whether they can combine a career and a family. The question of whether men should give up their jobs to have children, or whether in fact they can cope with both, never seems to arise.

There are many men who would agree with women that housework is a chore that benefits the whole family and that as such it ought to be shared. Many say they do share it, but often their share is less than they think. This may be because they just don't see what needs to be done. Unfortunately, many girls are brought up to 'see dust', whereas boys are expected to leave a trail of mess and dirty clothes behind them for their mothers to clear up, and this results in a discrepancy between the way in which women and men view housework. But a certain amount of order and cleanliness (as well as regular meals) is necessary for domestic comfort.

A recent study showed that for every two hours of housework a man does, a woman puts in five. Some men give

Togetherness

themselves a pat on the back for drying up the dishes and making breakfast at weekends. Generally, the attitude of men today is that they willingly 'help' around the house. And women whose partners participate in the housework are expected to be grateful for the 'help' they get. The word 'help' is significant, because it shows that housework is still regarded as the domain of women. Even if women don't do all the housework, they do tend to delegate it.

This causes problems for both parties. Women don't like having to ask men to hoover the floor and scrub out the lavatory: it causes stress and resentment. And it goes without saying that men don't like being asked to do chores: even if they don't find the chores demeaning, they don't like adopting the subordinate position of being asked or told to do them.

STAYING YOURSELF

When you become part of a couple there can be a tendency to merge identities. Both of you will probably have to adjust your routine and preferences slightly to accommodate the other. You may find yourself making compromises over matters of taste, in any area from music to wallpaper, and familiarity with the other person's opinions could convince you to adopt them as your own.

The danger is that your individuality could be submerged in conforming to shared standards and working towards shared goals. Partners are particularly at risk during the busy middle years of their marriage, when all their energy is directed into furthering ambitions at work, raising a family, and maintaining or improving their standard of living.

It takes more conscious effort to stay yourself if you are part of a couple. If you have no private time in which to pursue your own interests, or just to reflect on the important issues of your life, you may wake up one day wondering what has happened to the individual you once were. And if, in the mad dash to keep your household going and your family fed and schooled, you don't spend time relaxing with your partner, you may begin to ask yourself exactly who this person is who is sharing your life. Both of you are constantly changing and developing, but you will never find out how unless you give yourselves the chance to continue to get to know each other.

Coupledom need not be death to the individual. In fact the interest, support and encouragement of your partner can be just what you need in order to truly flourish. If you appreciate the fact that your personalities are complementary and not identical, then the differences as well as the similarities between you should act as catalysts to your own growth. In an atmosphere of mutual trust and liking, you can allow each other the freedom to continue with the individual pursuits you enjoyed before you moved in together, and to take up more interests, both personal and shared. Above all, you can carry on with the quest for self-knowledge and self-development by interacting with each other and confirming your understanding.

Understanding your partner

Sometimes misunderstandings arise in conversations between partners that can make you feel you are talking a different language.

In her book *You just don't understand*, American linguist Deborah Tannen explores the difference between the ways in which men and women use language, and the assumptions that lie behind the way they speak. As more equal rights and opportunities allow women to demonstrate their ability, and the New Man learns to change nappies, we may feel the sexes are becoming increasingly similar, but our approach to life is still gender-determined. We need to acknowledge the differences between the sexes in order to understand why our partners sometimes seem so unreasonable.

About 30 years ago, psychologists performed what became a famous experiment. Groups of men and women were asked to draw two circles, one representing themselves, and the other representing their relationship with their partner. The men drew two separate circles of equal size side by side on the page. The women's drawings showed more variety, but they all displayed a smaller circle representing the self, and a larger one representing the relationship; the two circles were always linked, sometimes overlapping, sometimes with the smaller circle completely enclosed inside the bigger one. This study showed how women see themselves as connected to the greater reality of their relationship, while men see themselves as standing apart, and set as much store by their independence as their relationship.

INBORN DIFFERENCES

Connectedness and independence are two traits that girls and boys develop early on in their playground games and conversations. Girls hold longer conversations with each other: they discuss their likes and dislikes and tell stories about their families and people they know. They tend to support and reinforce each other's opinions. The games they play involve cooperation.

Understanding your partner

Boys talk, or shout, in shorter bursts. What they say is often boastful ('I've got...') or challenging ('I bet you can't...'). Their games are rivalrous and often aggressive. However, girls act together as a network, nourishing individual friendships with long confiding talks; boys scramble for position in a hierarchy, always wanting to be one-up.

Attitudes developed during our childhood inform our adult behaviour in many ways. Women keep up a running dialogue with their female friends, exchanging small pieces of everyday news as well as bringing them up to date with their intimate thoughts and feelings. Men don't have comparable friendships with other men. They may discuss business strategy with colleagues, and perhaps there's banter in the pub after a game of squash (both types of conversation will have competitive elements), but talk about feelings among men is rare. A man may have a best male friend, whom he can consult in a crisis, but this is quite likely to be someone he doesn't see or speak to for months, even years, on end.

The reason men don't make a habit of opening up to male friends is that opening up makes you vulnerable, and men live in a hierarchical world where the vulnerable are quickly taken advantage of and put down. Therefore, status for men is crucial: they have to be seen by their peers to be important. This often involves what women think of as blowing their own trumpets.

Amongst women, it is not individual status that matters so much as being liked by their friends. Women don't feel comfortable blowing their own trumpets, because it would rock the boat of a friendship based on equality. In fact, when talking to other women, women tend to emphasize their failings rather than their successes. Failures are seen as more 'human', and they bring female

Understanding your partner

friends close in laughter, commiseration and sympathy.

So in conversation and relationships, women and men start from different viewpoints. The overall aim of women is to reach a consensus by discussion; the main aim of men is to make a pragmatic decision swiftly. The approach women adopt can seem annoyingly indirect and ineffectual to men; the approach men adopt sometimes appears unnecessarily aggressive and unfeeling to women.

The way women have learned to show caring is to put out their feelers, test the water and sympathetically suggest this and that, but men can interpret this as intrusive, even suffocatingly close. Men show caring in a different way. If a woman tells a man she has a problem, he is quite likely to either deny that it exists (*'Of course you'll pass the exam: now stop torturing yourself'*), or offer an instant solution (*'Well, if you fail you can always go back to temping'*). Both answers could cut a woman to the quick because they deny the complexity and indeed the validity of her feelings: they seem to crush and reject her. But the man has intended something completely different. With the first answer, *'Stop worrying'*, he meant to set her mind at rest; with the second, *'Go back to temping'*, he was offering a positive and practical alternative. However, what was meant as good advice by the man is interpreted by the woman as a slap in the face: she may feel it as a hurtful blow struck right at the very heart of the relationship.

Togetherness

READING BETWEEN THE LINES
Misunderstandings, such as the one described above, are commonplace between men and women and can cause lasting scars. It helps to learn to read between the lines and see the gender-influenced message behind the seemingly inappropriate words that your partner speaks. Here are some examples.

● Greg comes home from work on Friday night to find Anne preparing the dinner. '*Drop everything,*' he says. '*We're going for a Chinese with Alan and Barbara and some people they know.*' He thinks this will be a lovely surprise for Anne, who has had a tiring week. But Anne isn't pleased at all: she's worn out, and all she wants is a quiet evening at home. In fact she's not just disappointed, she's angry. '*Why did you arrange it without asking me?*' she wants to know. She would never presume to tell him to drop everything and come out with her friends; she even consults him before she makes an arrangement to go out on her own. It actually makes her feel good to tell her friends that she must check with Greg first, because it's a sign of how close they are.

An argument develops. She thinks he's inconsiderate and domineering. He retorts: '*But you can't expect me to tell Alan I have to ask my wife first, every time he asks me to go out. He'll think I haven't got a mind of my own.*'

Anne is saying: '*My way is to consult before arriving at a decision.*'

Greg is saying: '*I have to make a decision independently, or else I appear weak.*'

But Anne doesn't understand that Greg is operating within a hierarchy and can't afford to put himself in a subordinate position, and because they can't get to the root of their misunderstanding, the evening that Greg wanted to treat Anne to is ruined.

● Greg is having problems at work and complains of a persistent headache behind his eyes. '*I know exactly what that feels like,*' says Anne. '*It's exactly what I had when I had to mark all those examination papers last term.*' She means to offer him sympathy and support. But Greg doesn't see it like that. '*Why is it that whenever I say there's something wrong with me, then you've had it too?*' he snaps. '*You can't possibly know what I'm feeling. It's my headache, not yours.*'

Anne is hurt: his retort seems totally unreasonable. But to Greg, the fact that Anne claims experience of his headache detracts from the uniqueness of the pain he is feeling. In a hierarchy, possessions are important currency and demand to be defended. For Anne, from her female position in a network of support, sharing is more important than asserting sole ownership. Hearing him say, '*It's mine, not yours*', makes her feel cut off from him. It reminds her that when they are in company he often hurts her by referring to '*my house*', '*my car*', and even '*the day I got married*', when she would always say '*our*' and '*we*'.

● Anne and Greg go to a Spanish restaurant. The waiter arrives to take their order and Greg tells him that Anne speaks fluent Spanish. While Greg is listing Anne's linguistic achievements, the waiter's politeness barely hides his boredom; Anne is clearly embarrassed. After the waiter leaves, Anne gives Greg a ticking off: *'Why did you show me up like that? You made me feel like an idiot. You know my Spanish is useless – I certainly wasn't going to try it out in front of him.'*

Greg is really taken aback by the vehemence of Anne's protest. *'What are you talking about? You did really well in Spain last year. He would almost have taken you for a native.'* Greg is proud of Anne, and he wanted the waiter to be impressed by her. This is his way of giving recognition and support to his partner. But Anne doesn't see it like that: she sees it as boasting. And she doesn't feel that her Spanish is good enough to boast about. In a hierarchy, achievements are aired to announce status, but in a network, achievements make you stick out like a sore thumb, and lay you open to jealousy or ridicule.

COMMUNICATING ACROSS THE GENDER DIVIDE

If any of the misunderstandings described above strikes a chord with you, you will be bound to agree that there is a gender divide in the way we think and talk. It is natural for men to be concerned about maintaining their position in a hierarchy; natural for women to nurture their connections in a network. Both methods of approach have their advantages and their disadvantages, though since our society is still male-dominated, women's behaviour is all too often judged by the male standard, and found to be lacking.

Our dim view of female behaviour has permeated the language we use: for example, the word 'nag' is hardly ever applied to a man (see also Conflict, page 64). A woman may get labelled a nag if she repeatedly asks her man for cooperation ('Please do this or that for me', 'Please tell me how you feel'). A man may interpret a request to do something as an instruction, and since complying with an instruction means acknowledging an inferior position in a hierarchy, his instinct may tell him to refuse, thereby keeping his superior status. When the woman repeats her request, he calls her a nag. Thus a female drive, the desire to continue dialogue in order to connect, to cooperate, to understand each other and act as a team, is downgraded, and a row or an ugly silence may ensue.

However, the fact that there is a gender divide does not mean that we are doomed to go on misunderstanding each other. If partners can recognize the motive behind the message that jars, and allow for it, they will not be so irritated or hurt by each other. Learning each other's conversational approach will not put an end to disagreements, but it will help explain why the person you love can sometimes seem so thoughtless and alien. And talking about the motive behind the messages you send and receive can add a new dimension to understanding your partner.

Intimacy and sexual fulfilment

At the heart of every loving relationship is a closeness that offers deep satisfaction.

True emotional and sexual intimacy takes a long time to develop, and it is one of the major benefits of a long-term relationship that this should be so. The on-going process of getting to know each other is what keeps alive the fascination that brought you together in the first place.

Many couples miss out on this deeper level of intimacy. There is a common feeling that marriage kills sex, and that partners stop being 'in love' with each other after a couple of years of living together. They get tired of having sex with the same partner year after year, and boredom and gradual distancing create an atmosphere in which infidelity may be considered (see page 72). Marriage often comes to resemble a small, friendly business rather than a love affair.

If your relationship is securely founded in trust and promise, there is no reason why it should follow this course, provided that you nurture it rather than neglect it. Good sex happens between people who are intensely aware of each other's minds and bodies, and alive to each other's feelings. If you keep sight of one another's individuality and avoid settling into fixed and blinkered roles, your sex life should become ever more satisfying and lose none of its spontaneity and delight.

THE IMPORTANCE OF SHOWING AFFECTION

To hold your partner close in a tight, generous, all-enveloping hug is to affirm your acceptance of the way he or she is. Hugging, and other affectionate contact, such as holding hands, stroking, walking together arm in arm, or just sitting close, need not be sexual. Affectionate behaviour is more often loving, friendly, supportive, comforting, or just part of the fun of being together. But freely expressing your affection creates an atmosphere of physical ease between you and makes

Intimacy and sexual fulfilment

expressing and receiving sexuality easy and natural.

All physical contact is about learning each other's bodies, and knowing and understanding your partner's body – its responses as well as its contours – is essential for good sex. If you really know each other's bodies you will hardly ever move awkwardly in bed, jabbing each other with elbows and knees, twisting arms and leaning painfully on long hair. You may be surprised at how well your bodies mould together, at the fluidity of your movements, and at the warm glow afterwards, where with a previous partner whom you knew and loved less well you might have experienced aching muscles. Good lovemaking is relaxing and blissfully comfortable, and has its roots in easy affectionate behaviour. People who learn about each other's bodies through closeness and physical affection can tell the minute a loving hug melts into an erotic one. Lovemaking develops spontaneously and naturally as they discover each other's sexual response.

Women love to be caressed, to share warmth and closeness in bed, to snuggle up and talk quietly, and to fall asleep with bodies entwined. But some men have difficulty with this area of sexuality. They are inhibited about showing affection, preferring to get straight down to the business of having sex. The mechanistic approach hurts women: if sex doesn't involve affection they feel used, and afterwards discarded.

Men who don't naturally show affection complain that they don't like women 'hanging round' them; hugging and kissing is something they tolerate only if sex is the reward. Inhibitions about expressing affection are rooted in the way boys are brought up to believe that cuddling and kissing are 'childish' or 'not masculine'. Male skin, like female skin, is highly sensitive and responsive, an erogenous zone that covers the whole body, and the unaffectionate man is missing out by not recognizing it. If your man is reluctant to show affection, get him to relax and then give him a massage (see page 130) to show him just how luxurious it can be to succumb to the attention of someone who cares. Then ask him to do the same for you.

Sometimes men complain that women who want affection for its own sake fail to take into account the ease with which they, men, get sexually aroused. If a woman arouses a man, and then pushes him away, he is likely to feel frustration and anger. Again, the solution is to be sensitive to one another's needs. It is important not to draw a line between affection and sex, or to put your feelings in boxes: although it is possible to feel affectionate without feeling sexy, sex grows out of affection, and affection is part of sex. Our feelings can't be turned on and off at will, as if by flicking a switch. It is ignorant and hurtful for a man who behaves coldly to a woman all day to expect her to be hot the minute they get into bed, and it is equally ignorant and hurtful for a woman to inflame a man and then, when he wants sex, to leap away as though she has been burned. A couple who are physically and mentally in touch can sense the degrees of affection and sexuality as they develop, and go with them, if the time is right, or check them without rejection, but with the promise of later fulfilment if the time is wrong.

SHARING SEXUAL RESPONSIBILITY

The advent of the Pill in the 1960s and the publication of the first studies into female sexuality launched women into a new era of sexual freedom. They realized their capacity for pleasure, and they discovered how to get it. Some feminists were quick to blame men for holding them back sexually, and the stereotype of the Male Chauvinist Pig was born. An exploitative bigot, in bed the MCP cared only for his own sexual satisfation and had intercourse without arousing his partner or bringing her to orgasm.

Since that time men have become far more aware that selfishness cripples relationships and means missing out on a whole spectrum of sexual sensation. So if your man doesn't satisfy you, don't dismiss him as insensitive when he may just be embarrassed or ignorant of the possibilities; show him what you enjoy and teach him how to do it for you.

Sharing sexual responsibility means being equal partners in making love. Gone are the days when it was considered 'fast' for women to take the initiative in sex, but it seems they still lag behind. A recent survey showed that heterosexual and gay male couples have sex more frequently than lesbian couples, indicating that women are still reluctant to take the lead. Good sex is sex without inhibitions, and that means not holding back when you want something. Being spontaneous, imaginative and inventive is part of the fun of making love, and both partners lose out if the woman regularly lies back and lets it 'be done' to her. Good sex is an engagement of minds and bodies: it happens when both partners participate to the full.

Another responsibility that should be shared is protection, against both pregnancy and disease. Exclusive sexual partners should not have to worry about infection, although there are some sexually transmitted diseases that can occur spontaneously (see page 61), without either of you being unfaithful. If you are having an affair, one of the worst ways your partner can find out about it is by catching an infection, because of course the feeling of degradation is compounded by the disease. A condom is the best protection against AIDS and other venereal diseases.

You may decide to change your contraception methods from time to time, as there are advantages and disadvantages to each method. Although it is the most effective contraceptive known, the Pill does not suit all women, and even those in whom it produces no adverse side effects may not like the idea of tampering chemically with the delicate balance of their hormones. However, for some women, the Pill not only affords effortless protection, but also minimizes the discomfort of periods.

Togetherness

Mechanical methods such as the condom and the cap have the obvious disadvantage that they involve literally putting a barrier between the partners, and this can have an inhibiting effect. Condom manufacturers suggest that women should put on their partners' condoms to avoid breaking the momentum of lovemaking.

New contraceptives, such as the sponge and the female condom, are coming on to the market all the time, and for a complete review of these and other methods, such as the coil or IUD, and vasectomy or sterilization, you can visit your local family planning clinic for free consultation and advice.

INTIMACY

It has been said that the mind is our most important sex organ: the best sex happens when partners consciously engage with each other's minds as well as bodies. The dynamism will start to drain from your relationship if you let sex become a routine that you perform with half your attention elsewhere. If you aren't feeling like sex, it's much better to say so and cuddle up close until you fall asleep, rather than enduring the attentions of your partner out of habit or a sense of obligation.

Sex is not about fulfilling a contract or proving yourself. It is not a duty or competition, but an opportunity for sharing your feelings. No other activity gives such intense awareness of living in the present. Many sex books stress the importance of variety in keeping your interest in sex alive. Sometimes they give the impression that flagging passion can be rekindled by deciding to try a new position, or by having sex on the sofa instead of in bed, or by wearing silk and drinking champagne. But no amount of inventiveness can work if the feeling is not there in the first place. The richest variety that you can bring to your sex life comes from within yourself.

The true meaning of 'intercourse' is 'dealings in which there is an exchange of communication'. What you are communicating is the way you feel, and this is constantly changing. Sex will always be different if you see it as a means of self-expression. It can be playful, adventurous, erotic. It allows for many moods to express themselves one after the other: passion, tenderness, lust, and mischievous curiosity. And an open aproach to making love also allows other things to happen in bed besides sex: it encourages talk and laughter. In bed you can bare your soul to your partner as well as your body. You are free to shed your inhibitions and be quite simply yourself.

However, 'being yourself' is not always as easy as it should be. The idea of 'being uninhibited' and 'letting go' represents chaos and disaster if you have been brought up to believe that keeping control is the key to survival and success in life. The fear of what might happen – perhaps you might be overtaken by a sort of madness or mindless passion – if you do let go in bed, can result in a relationship in which you never give yourself fully to your partner. Part of you always feels that it's holding back. This reserve may not stop you having orgasms, but it will leave you with the feeling that sex is a threat to something deep inside yourself and that you have to defend yourself gainst it. And not being able to give yourself will leave you feeling disappointed and unfulfilled – as if sex has cheated you, and has turned out to be a lot of fuss about nothing.

Both men and women who are afraid of letting go in bed fake passion and orgasm, but men can usually disguise it better: it's less easy to tell if they are only 'going through the motions', because erection and ejaculation are 'proof' of their sexuality. A woman who wants to express passion but can't let go often resorts to acting, hoping to convince her partner by behaving like a star in a blue movie. Acting in bed is an exhausting and lonely business. You are at your most vulnerable, and in need of warmth and closeness, but what results is cold, mechanical sex. It is deeply unsatisfying, because it erects a barrier of misunderstanding between you and your partner, and if the problem is not tackled soon, it will simply drive you further apart.

SHEDDING YOUR INHIBITIONS

So what is 'uninhibited'? Acting uninhibited is a far cry from being uninhibited, which is first and foremost being oneself. It is the very simplest thing, and yet, to the sexually inhibited, the most difficult.

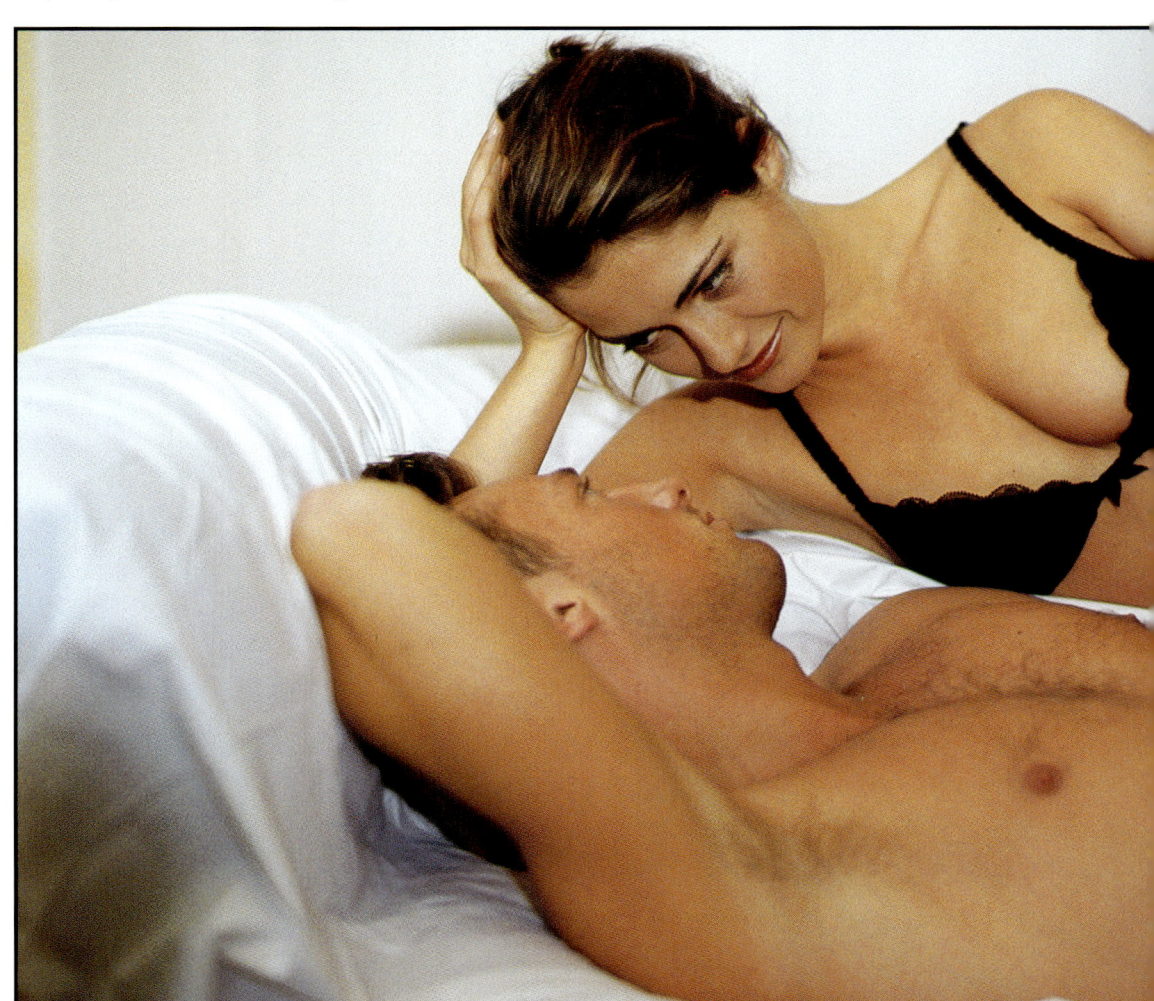

Intimacy and sexual fulfilment

The first step towards getting rid of your inhibitions is to relax. This is also often easier said than done. If told to relax, your partner may well reply through gritted teeth that he or she *is* relaxed. The best way to relax is to try and stop thinking of sex as a performance. You are not on show. This is a private act, just between the two of you, and no one is sitting in judgment to give you marks out of ten. You are not out to achieve anything. Too many people are anxious about the climax before they begin. The man may be worried about losing his erection, the woman about not having an orgasm. Forget all that. Pleasure lies in the present, and you must live for the moment if you are to enjoy it.

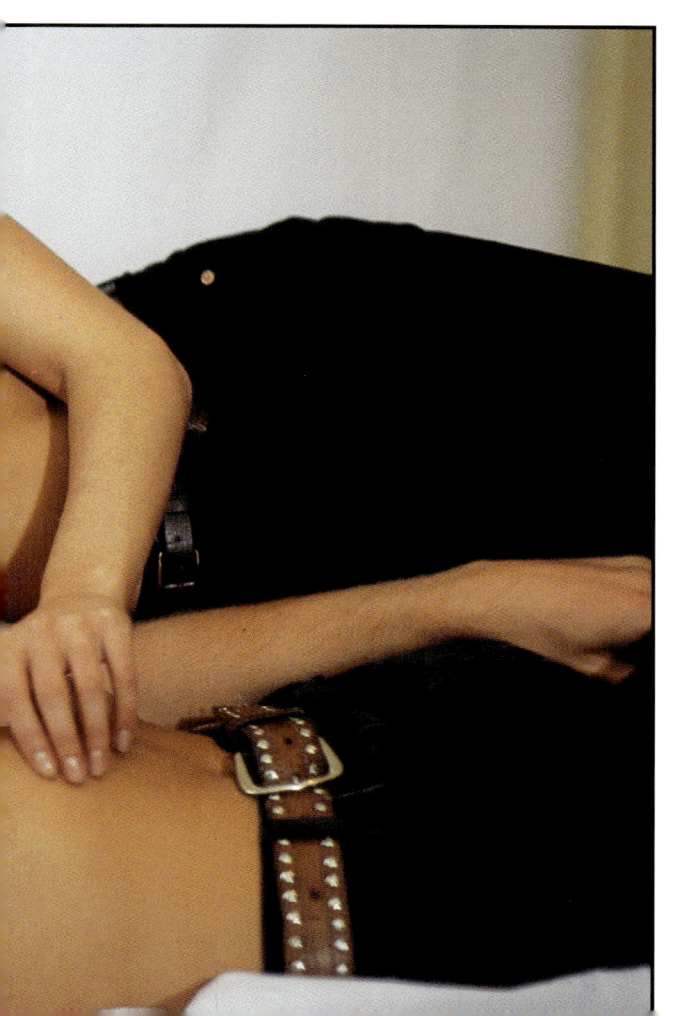

Allow yourselves unlimited time and absolute privacy. Take things extremely slowly, savouring each touch and caress. Don't force anything, and if one of you feels that the other has made an artificial move – one that smacks of 'getting on with it' – gently stop him or her from continuing and re-establish your bearings. Being uninhibited is doing what you both like, and you are finding out exactly what that is, by moving very tentatively, as if you are exploring each other's bodies for the first time. Most of us like tenderness and gentleness; few like things they find unnatural or bizarre. Most people are touched by the admission of vulnerablity, and touched by caring. So there is no need to be frightened. There is no possibility that you will suddenly lose control, because you are moving so very slowly, and paying so much attention to each other.

Many people fear passion because, having experienced it only in their imagination, they think it will turn them into harlots or rapists. So they decide consciously to control it. By the time they meet somebody they really like, they may be accomplished in the mechanics of sex, but the ability to feel has been buried. In order to get the full potential out of your relationship, you must throw away your inhibitions. This involves not putting on an act, but stripping yourself bare of all pretence, and learning your own sexuality and that of your partner with all the curiosity and excitement and tenderness that you wish you had experienced when you lost your virginity.

Solving sexual problems

Sexuality between two people is a living thing, and like the rest of your relationship it is bound to go through periods of fallowness and troughs as well as peaks of excitement.

When your love life is less than sparkling, try not to blame yourself or your partner. Problems start when dissatisfaction with less-than-perfect sex turns inwards and a destructive emotional cycle begins. If your body does not respond as you would like, self-doubt and anxiety can make it even less responsive. Fears mount up all too easily, and suddenly your whole sexual identity can seem under threat.

The good news is that there is a very simple solution for the vast majority of sexual problems, because most of them are psychological, and caused by stress. In order to enjoy sex with your partner you both need to be fully relaxed. Only then can you float out of time and become totally absorbed in the fluid world of sensation and emotion. Memories and expectations fall away, and you live fully in the present. Making love can be the most complete experience, but it is as fragile as it is beautiful, and demands and pressures from outside can easily burst the bubble and return you to earth with a thud.

THE PRESSURES THAT CAN CAUSE PROBLEMS

While you're making love, distractions can come in the form of a knock at the door, or a stray thought surfacing: 'Must buy pet food.' This kind of interruption is annoying, but usually causes no more than a very temporary loss of arousal. However, more insistent pressures, such as business not finished, deadlines not met, bills not paid, can cause physical and mental tension to build up to the extent that you just cannot give yourself to lovemaking at all. An even more common cause for lack of sexual response is a temporary lack of rapport with your partner. Perhaps you feel angry or resentful over something that happened between you, or doubt your partner's love. Maybe your partner is putting too many de-

Solving sexual problems

mands on you and making you feel under pressure to 'perform'. In both men and women, stress can cause sexual apathy, and apathy is a big turn-off for your partner. However, a person under stress can still want to make love, but find their body lets them down. For women, this may mean that though they go through all the motions of making love, they lose the power to feel and react, and orgasms become infrequent or cease altogether. Men may have problems with erection or ejaculation, or both. Often a man under stress can't get an erection at all, or else it wilts as soon as he tries to penetrate his partner. He may ejaculate immediately he enters her, or may even have difficulty ejaculating at all.

These problems are dealt with individually below, but an important factor in the resolution of any sexual difficulty lies in the way you and your partner approach it. Patience, understanding and a suspension of demand are the key elements that allow recovery. Overleaf are some useful guidelines.

TAKING THE THREAT OUT OF SEXUAL DIFFICULTIES

1 First of all, don't blame your body if it doesn't respond as you would wish. Physical and sexual responses cannot be activated on demand, they are part of your very complex and sensitive emotional make-up. If your body is not responding, it doesn't mean that there is something physically wrong with you. Lack of sexual response is a sign that you are under stress. Learn to trust your body and to read its signals.

2 Find the cause of your stress. You may know what it is, or you may not have even realized you were under stress. We often hide from ourselves problems we don't want to face, so discovering the cause may not be easy. Ask yourself whether you LIKE *your partner. Not love her,* LIKE *her. Are you angry or resentful? Are you feeling insecure after a period of abstinence, such as after the birth of a baby?*

3 Talk with your partner about what makes you uneasy, angry or resentful, so that together you can crystallize the problem. Problems lose much of their burden once they have been pinpointed, because then you can work out how to deal with them. If there is no easy solution, at least you can discuss how to best cope. Life will never be problem-free, but identifying and dealing with problems will free you from the stress that builds up when you try to ignore them or shut them out of the bedroom.

4 Don't say yes when you mean no. If you try to make love when you don't really feel like it just to please your partner, you can't expect your body to respond. Both of you will end up disappointed. Men as well as women have times when what they want is not sex, but just to be held close. Tell your partner if you just want to be hugged. This inspires more trust than saying you do want to make love and then proving you don't.

5 Take the perfunctoriness out of sex. Don't just leap into bed and expect instant erection and lubrication: this is the stuff of pornography, not life. Relax together: cuddle on the bed in your clothes, talking about your day. Massage knots of tension from each other's necks. Undress slowly. Perhaps take a warm shower together. Allow time to unravel the tensions of the day and leave them behind before you get into bed.

6 Take the pressure off yourself to 'perform'. The competitive spirit has no place in the bedroom. Sex is not about scoring goals, reaching targets or breaking records; it's not about proving yourself or impressing anyone else. Making love is a private communication between just the two of you: it's about how you feel; it's about enjoying physical contact. Don't force yourself to follow a set menu in your lovemaking. Talk to your partner about it and allow yourselves to do as much or as little as you want.

WOMEN AND DIFFICULTIES WITH ORGASM

During the '80s women were put under a lot of pressure to have orgasms. But the more deliberately she is coaxed to come, the more self-conscious a woman can become and the harder she feels she must try: often with the result that she has no orgasm at all.

Female orgasm is caused by stimulation of the clitoris, and the clitoris does not usually receive much stimulation during penetration, which is why only a minority of women orgasm with their partner's penis inside them. The best way for a man to give his partner an orgasm is to gently play with her clitoris with his fingers (masturbation) or tongue (cunnilingus). Freud and his followers caused a lot of anguish to women by calling this kind of orgasm 'immature', and orgasm with penetration 'mature'. However, clinical research since Freud has shown that there is in fact only one type of female orgasm. An orgasm is an orgasm, and it doesn't matter how you have it, only that it feels good. An orgasm with fingers or tongue feels exquisitely sweet and acute; if the penis is inside the vagina when the woman comes, the orgasm feels muffled, like a dull explosion, but it's the same experience.

You need to give your partner plenty of time to get aroused before you touch her genitals. Show her how you feel by the way you look at her and in your voice; kiss her and caress her all over. Ask her how she would like you to stimulate her: with your fingers or tongue; directly on her clitoris, or tantalizingly near it; firmly, or lightly and with just the gentlest flicking movement. Be prepared to carry on for a long time: if she thinks you're going to back off she will tense up. If she loses the feeling, she can tell you to stop.

ADVICE FOR MEN

- *Most men like the look, smell and taste of their partner's vagina, but most women still need to be reassured that this is so.*
- *Don't penetrate your partner unless and until she's fully lubricated. You can buy jellies for this purpose (the Pill and ageing tend to cause dryness), but her own juices (from arousal) or your saliva (from cunnilingus) are better.*
- *Some women like to come more than once in a lovemaking session, but in many more, the clitoris becomes too sensitive to touch after orgasm: don't ever push your partner to come – it could make her feel as though she's taking part in a laboratory experiment.*
- *If you have to ask 'Did you come?' it puts a woman on the spot and makes her feel a failure either way. If she didn't, she feels inadequate, and if she did, it's pretty humiliating that you didn't notice. If you don't know how to recognize orgasm in your partner, it probably means that you are not used to giving her cunnilingus: try it, and you'll see and feel what female orgasm is like. If you think she might have come while you were inside her, but don't want to risk the question, try putting it another way: 'What would you like me to do for you now?', for example.*

Togetherness

- If your partner says she doesn't want to make love, offer her plenty of reassuring affection instead. Respect her feelings, remembering that there is only a thin line between persuasion and coercion.

ADVICE FOR WOMEN

- Most women are capable of orgasm, and most can discover the pleasure of orgasm through masturbation. Once you have learned how to masturbate, you can teach your partner how to do it for you. Experiment to see what kind of caresses you enjoy giving yourself, using your fingers or a dildo and a cream or lotion if you like. Take your time, and don't expect to reach orgasm during your first session; if masturbating is a new experience you may not feel comfortable with it straight away.

DIFFICULTIES WITH ERECTION

There are times during lovemaking when erection will subside, and then get stronger again. This is perfectly natural and should not bother you or your partner. However, if your penis refuses to get hard at all, or flops as soon as you attempt penetration, it can be both distressing and humiliating. And if it happens repeatedly it's possible to imagine that you are not just out of touch sexually, but also losing your grip emotionally and even mentally.

Of course, there are no grounds for such fears. There are many causes of non-erection, and most of them are psychological and stress-related (see above). Follow the advice on page 52 (Taking the threat out of sexual difficulties). It's important to be able to talk to your partner about this, as she will want the problem to clear up as much as you do. She may be worried that you have gone off her. Reassure her that this is not so, but try to explore any difficulties that there might be between you. The worst thing you can do is to retreat into moodiness, sulk, or blame.

ADVICE FOR MEN

- Environmental pollutants can cause erection problems, as can diabetes and alcohol. One or two drinks can be relaxing and sexually liberating; a few more can leave you with the desire, but not the ability; and more still can drug you into a stupor. Erection problems are common among alcoholics.
- Age is another factor to consider. Older men don't get erect as quickly as younger men, and the erection may not be quite as hard. This is not a problem: older men have many years of experience behind them and can therefore be the most skillful and imaginative lovers. They can usually make love for longer than younger men, though they need longer periods in between lovemaking sessions before they are capable of another erection.
- Men are sometimes so ashamed of being limp that they blame their partners for their non-erection. Although you may well have problems with your relationship, the fact that you can't get an erection is never directly anyone's fault, yours or hers. Blaming it on your partner's looks ('You're too fat to turn me on') is as cruel as it's unrealistic, and blame is always

destructive. However, if your partner is unresponsive, and makes you feel you are 'doing all the work', then you have got into a situation where neither of you is turning the other on, and a bit more input from her can definitely help. Tell her your feelings and show her how you would like her to arouse you. Seeing you excited will excite her too, and the circle will have been broken.

ADVICE FOR WOMEN

- *It's easy to feel rejected if your partner repeatedly presents you with a limp penis: don't, because it's not your fault.*
- *Don't keep trying to stimulate an unresponsive penis. Instead, give your partner lots of reassurance and affection, but keep it light: heavy sympathy will intensify his feeling of failure. Make it clear that there are other ways in which he can satisfy you. Asking him to do so can give him his confidence back.*
- *If it happens repeatedly there's no point ignoring it in the hope that it will go away. If he doesn't broach the subject, you must, for your own sake as well as his. Probing delicately, try to discover the stress that's causing the problem, and get him to talk about it.*
- *Take the pressure off him to have intercourse, and spend as much time as you can just relaxing together.*

DIFFICULTIES WITH EJACULATION

There are no rules about how long intercourse should last before a man ejaculates. The Taoists of Ancient China advised that men should conserve semen, which they thought of as being the 'life force', and ejaculate as infrequently as possible. However, today, non-ejaculation can be seen as a problem. In fact, it's perfectly natural for older men not to ejaculate every time they make love, and non-ejaculation enables them to make love more frequently, as it may take several days for an older man to get another erection after he has ejaculated.

Non-ejaculation can be distressing in younger men. As with other sexual difficulties, the causes are almost always psychological. Suppressed anger towards your partner might be causing you to withhold ejaculation. Examine your feelings closely to see where the problem lies. Often, men who don't ejaculate come from strict religious backgrounds or otherwise sexually repressive families. If this is true of you and you have a long-term problem with ejaculation, then there is no doubt that counselling could help. Ring your local Relate or marriage guidance office to obtain more details of appropriate services in your area.

Many men experience what is known as 'premature ejaculation', i.e. they ejaculate just before or immediately after penetration. The problem lies in the fact that early ejaculation is usually involuntary, but not always, as sometimes coming quickly is an expression of immense excitement and emotional urgency. Men who repeatedly ejaculate involuntarily can get very depressed with their lack of control and become convinced that there is something seriously wrong with them; however, premature ejaculation is not a

Solving sexual problems

disease but a habit, and, like any other habit, it can be unlearned. Sexologists have developed two sets of simple exercises that have helped many thousands of men to last longer (see pages 58–59).

● *The most likely cause of involuntary ejaculation is stress. Ask yourself if there is any reason why you should want to get lovemaking over with as quickly as possible. Are you feeling insecure or resentful towards your partner? Are you feeling guilty about something? Are other problems distracting you? Try following the steps for stress-free lovemaking* (*Taking the threat out of sexual difficulties, see page 52*).

● *Men who ejaculate involuntarily are often concerned that they don't last long enough to satisfy their partner. Since the majority of women don't come with their partner's penis inside them, this should not be a problem. You can bring your partner to orgasm with your fingers or tongue before you penetrate her. Once you have come, relax together for as long as it takes until you get a second erection: the second time round you are likely to be able to last longer, especially if you move slowly and gently.*

Techniques for Lasting Longer

Stop-start

This is a sequence of exercises designed by Dr James Semans to help the large number of men who ejaculate immediately they enter or touch their partner's vagina with their penis, or even before. The aim of the exercises is to learn to keep yourself below the point at which ejaculation seems inevitable for as long as possible. The first three steps can be practised without your partner to help you gain a greater measure of control. For the final four steps you will need your partner's cooperation.

- *STEP ONE* Masturbate with a dry hand. Avoid fantasizing, and concentrate instead on the sensation in your penis. Allow the pleasure to build up but stop immediately you feel you are about to lose control. Relax for a while, until the danger of ejaculation has passed, then begin again. Following the same pattern, aim to continue stopping and starting for 15 minutes without orgasm. You may not be able to manage it at first, but keep trying. As you get more practised, you will probably find you have to stop less often. When you have completed three 15-minute sessions on consecutive occasions (not necessarily one immediately after the other!), proceed to step two.

- *STEP TWO* Masturbate with a lubricating jelly, which will heighten sensation, and make ejaculation more difficult to delay. Follow the technique in step one for three 15-minute sessions.

- *STEP THREE* You will now have gained a good measure of control. The next step involves masturbating with a dry hand without stopping for 15 minutes before ejaculation. Keep focusing on your penis rather than fantasizing. When you feel yourself getting dangerously excited, don't stop, but instead, change rhythm or alter your strokes in such a way that the pressure to ejaculate fades. Experiment to see which strokes excite you most, and which allow you most control. Work on this until you have completed three sessions.

- *STEP FOUR* Now involve your partner. Lie on your back and get her to masturbate you with a dry hand, as in step one. Concentrate on the sensations in your penis and ask her to stop every time you get too aroused before the 15 minutes is up. Aim to last for three sessions.

- *STEP FIVE* Repeat step four, but ask your partner to use a lubricant while she masturbates you. You will find ejaculation much more difficult to control, and you may have to ask her to stop more often. Once you have mastered three 15-minute sessions, you are ready to try the technique with intercourse.

- *STEP SIX* The best position for delaying ejaculation is with the woman on top. Once you are inside her, ask her to move gently. Put your hands on her hips so that you can signal when you want her to stop, and when to start again. Again, aim to last for 15 minutes, but if you can't, don't worry: you can start again once you have recovered your erection, and the second time around you'll probably have more control. During intercourse, concentrate entirely on yourself. Give your partner your full concentration and bring her to orgasm either before or afterwards, with your fingers or tongue.

● *STEP SEVEN* Move on to other positions, noting that it is more difficult to delay ejaculation with the man on top.

THE SQUEEZE

This technique was developed by the American sex experts Masters and Johnson to help men who ejaculate too soon, and it often succeeds where the stop-start technique fails. In fact, Masters and Johnson found that it helped 98 per cent of the men for whom they prescribed it.

The 'squeeze' action is designed to cause your erection to subside, and it is applied every time you get too close to ejaculation. Your partner performs the squeeze by gripping your penis firmly, and pressing with her thumb on the frenulum. This is the place on the underside of the penis where the head joins the shaft. At the same time, she presses on the opposite side of the penis with her forefinger, and with her other fingers curled around the shaft. It is important that she presses fairly hard on the penis and doesn't move her hand while doing so. Too light a touch and any movement could be too stimulating and cause you to ejaculate straight away.

● *STEP ONE* Get your partner to masturbate you with a dry hand. Any time you get too close to ejaculation, signal to her to stop and squeeze your penis. Aim to last for three consecutive 15-minute sessions before moving on to step two.

● *STEP TWO* Get your partner to masturbate you, but this time use a lubricant. Follow the procedure for step one.

● *STEP THREE* Now you are ready for intercourse, but not for thrusting. Instead, lie on your back and ask your partner to sit on top of you, with your penis inside her. Neither of you should move. As soon as you feel the urge to come, your partner should rise off you (be careful as this applies stimulation), and immediately hold your penis in the squeeze grip. Repeat the exercise a couple of times before you allow yourself to ejaculate.

● *STEP FOUR* When you feel more confident about your self-control, ask your partner to move gently while she sits on top of you in the same position. When you feel the urge to ejaculate, she should move off you and squeeze as before until you can last for 15 minutes.

● *STEP FIVE* You are now ready to try other positions but remember that with the man on top, you will have least control. As with the stop-start technique, keep your attention on yourself. Your partner will not feel neglected if you bring her to orgasm with your tongue or fingers either before or after intercourse.

Faking it

Both men and women may fake orgasm. They do it because they feel if they don't come they are somehow inadequate, and don't want to admit it, or because they want to bring lovemaking that they are no longer enjoying to an end. Faking orgasm is always destructive, because it puts a barrier of deceit and mistrust between you and your partner. Bed is the place where you should be able to be most intimate, which means being most vulnerable, most honest and, above all, most truly yourself.

So don't feel obliged to make love if you don't want to. Explain to your partner how you feel. You should get rid of the idea that sex is a performance with standards that have to be lived up to. There is nothing wrong if you don't have an orgasm: take off the pressure and just enjoy the pleasure of the present sensation.

SEXUALLY TRANSMITTED DISEASES

The discovery of a tender red place, spot or swelling on your genitals can lead to the instant fear that your partner has been unfaithful and has passed on to you a sexually transmitted disease caught in an adulterous relationship. Of course it is possible that this may have happened, but you shouldn't jump to conclusions.

First, your symptom may be no more than the kind of spot or itchy red place that you might develop on the skin anywhere else on your body; on your face, for instance. One of the tiny ducts under the skin may have become blocked, or you may have caused a spot to form by accidentally pulling out a pubic hair.

Another possibility is that you have an infection that is indeed sexually transmitted, but which may occur spontaneously without any change of sex partner, such as NSU (non-specific urethritis), thrush, or genital warts. There are simple treatments for all of these diseases, but of course they need to be taken by both partners in order to avoid reinfection. Another disease that can be passed backwards and forwards between partners is genital herpes (see page 63), which is a more distressing condition.

If you suspect that you may have a sexually transmitted disease, your first step should be to discuss it with your partner, bearing in mind that it might just be a spot or a spontaneously occurring infection, and your next step should be to visit a special clinic together to have some tests carried out. Both you and your partner will need to be treated.

The telephone number of your nearest genito-urinary clinic (also called 'special clinic') will be available from your local hospital or family planning clinic. You will be seen as soon as possible, and specially trained staff will do everything they can to put you at your ease. Your visit and any treatment will be completely confidential.

The doctor will need to ask some questions about your sexual practices. There is no need to feel guilt or shame: he or she will be a sympathetic and professional clinician, and not out to apportion blame. A nurse will usually explain the examination procedure and prepare you for any tests. Women usually have an internal examination, which can feel uncomfortable but not painful. Discomfort is more often psychological than physical. Swabs are taken from the vagina and cervix (neck of the womb). Some of the samples may be tested immediately, while others will probably be sent off to a laboratory, in which case the results will be ready in about 10 days.

Special clinics do not routinely test for AIDS. If you want to know more about this, or any other sexually transmitted disease, ask for an information sheet at the clinic or see your doctor.

● NSU, NON-SPECIFIC URETHRITIS, is also called NGU, non-gonoccocal urethritis. Sometimes there are no symptoms with this disease, but if they do manifest themselves, they are likely to take the form of a discharge from the vagina, penis or anus, or some itching or soreness around the genitals or anus, or a lump or rash on the genitals, anus or mouth. The treatment is usually a two-week course of antibiotics. During the course of treatment, patients are asked to give up drinking alcohol, as this can make symptoms recur. Complications can occur with NSU, but early diagnosis and treatment can prevent these.

● GENITAL WARTS are unpleasant but painless small lumps that can appear spontaneously on the penis, vulva or anus and are mildly contagious. Treatment involves either painting the warts with a preparation called podophyllin, which can be done at home, or freezing them off with liquid nitrogen. An association has been identified between genital warts and cervical cancer, so it is important to get rid of them promptly and to have regular cervical smears.

● THRUSH is a fungal infection that develops in certain conditions in the vagina.

Solving sexual problems

baths, and wearing tights, tight jeans and nylon knickers.

● GENITAL HERPES is a viral infection, one of a family that also includes cold sores. In fact it can be caught by having oral sex with a partner who has active cold sores. The symptoms are itching, pain in the groin, discomfort on urinating and fever, followed by the appearance of painful red blisters on the vulva or penis, which burst to form ulcers.

After about 10 days the symptoms disappear and the patient appears to be cured. But the infection is only lying dormant and may recur at any time, particularly when the patient is under stress. There is as yet no treatment for this disease, although the drug Acyclovir relieves symptoms and reduces the duration of attacks. The doctor may also prescribe bed rest, with some paracetamol for the pain and a saline bath for the affected area.

During the dormant phase of the disease, it is safe to have sex without infecting your partner, but it is impossible to predict when the next attack may occur, so the risk of infection remains. If the infection is active at the end of a pregnancy, a Caesarian section may be performed to prevent the baby becoming infected in the birth canal.

Genital herpes is a very painful and distressing disease that has reached epidemic proportions in America. The good news is that it does sometimes burn itself out, and that the prospect of an eventual cure looks promising.

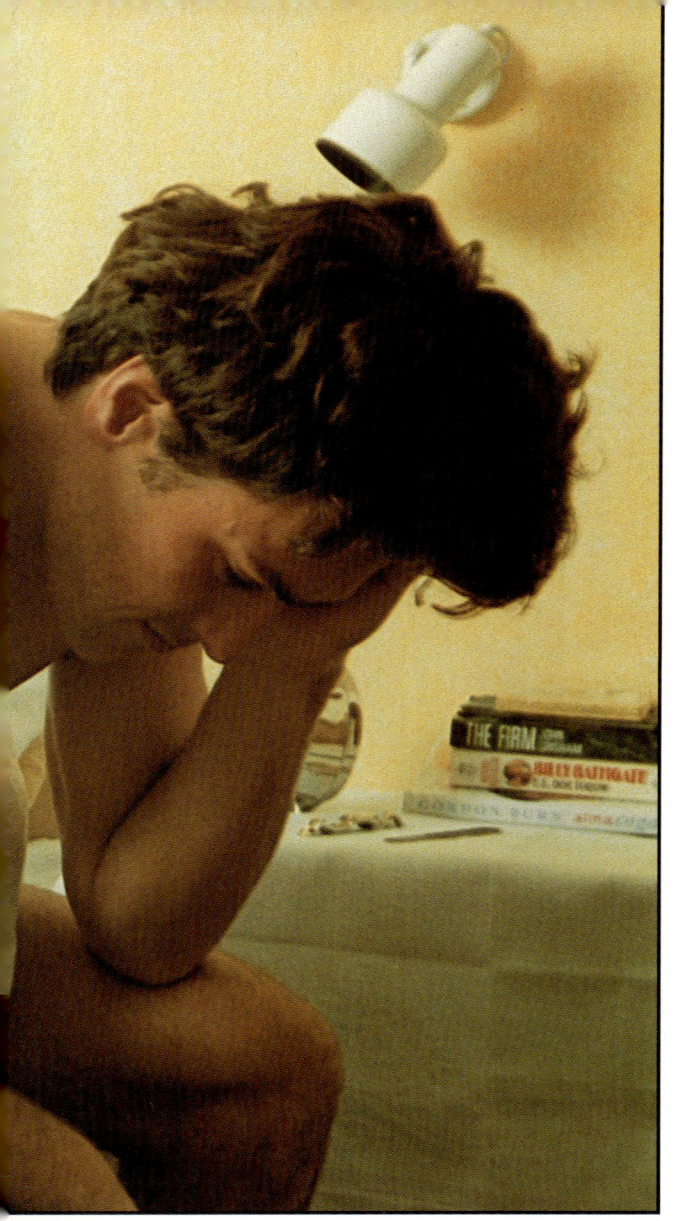

It is sometimes linked to taking the Pill, and if it recurs frequently, a different method of contraception may be advisable. A man may carry thrush, although he usually manifests no symptoms. Thrush causes vaginal soreness and itching, and a thick white discharge. The doctor will prescribe anti-fungal cream, to be used by both partners, and vaginal pessaries, although oral treatments are available too. Some women find that natural yoghurt introduced into the vagina on a tampon is effective. Avoid hot

Conflict

When you fall in love, it seems impossible to imagine arguing with your partner. But the better you get to know each other, the clearer and more irritating the differences between you become.

Being in love makes you feel indulgent, as if you could cope with anything. This state of affairs is not likely to last for long. However much your views coincide, your approach to the relationship is bound not to be identical. In the mix of differences and similarities between you lies not only the richness and excitement of being together, but also the source of potential conflict. Conflict is an area that frightens many people. Dreading the destructive power of anger unleashed, they go out of their way to avoid it. So what do they do when something annoys them? They bite back the annoyance, and instead of tackling the problem directly, they convey their feelings by sulking, brooding and 'moods'. They belligerently withdraw their attention from each other. Does your partner hide behind the paper or in the toolshed? Slump in front of the television? Do you go off into another room, slamming the door behind you?

Cutting off communication like this produces two results. In the short term it makes you feel isolated and resentful, and it does not solve the problem, which will therefore recur. In the long term, a build-up of silences, moods and unresolved problems will cause you to fall out of love. The main problem in love relationships is caused not by conflict, which is inevitable, but by the way in which we handle it. People who refuse to handle it at all in the hope that it will just melt away, are acting like ostriches. Does conflict have to be as destructive and harmful as the ostrich imagines? Or could it be that identifying a problem and arguing it through leads to increased understanding and closeness between partners? Can arguing after all play a positive role in an intimate relationship?

How men and women handle conflict

Men and women tend to handle conflict differently, according to the 4,500 women who answered Shere Hite's questionnaires for compilation in her *Report on Love, Passion and Emotional Violence* (1987).

Women are brought up to be loving

Conflict

and caring: they need, and are able to provide, a rich emotional life. Because they are so good at empathizing, they are quick to detect even slightly jarring off-notes or absences of response from their partners; because they are so good at expressing their feelings, they are able to voice the negative (as well as the positive) in their own reactions. They need to say what is wrong in order to restore harmony to the relationship.

Unfortunately, most men are not so well attuned to their partners: their emotional radar is undeveloped because they have been brought up to believe that feeling is messy and gets in the way of doing. Emotions are what women have: they signify weakness and being out of control. Boys are taught that openly showing distress and affection is soppy. They learn to suppress their feelings to the point where they actually don't recognize they have them. (It is not unusual for a man whose behaviour shows that he loves deeply to be able to say that he doesn't really know what love is.) If men don't recognize feelings in themselves, they are hardly likely to be able to detect subtle shifts of emotion in their partners.

When a woman confronts a man with an emotional problem, the man is likely to be mystified: 'I don't know what you're talking about. Everything's quite alright as far as I'm concerned,' is a common response. Arguments often develop like this: the woman explains the problem; the man is baffled. The woman, frustrated that her partner can't see what is plainly obvious to her, explains again, in stronger terms; the man again denies the problem exists. The woman, feeling quite rightly that her words are not getting through, shouts to make herself heard: the man accuses her of getting all worked up without any cause, getting 'too emotional' over 'nothing'.

This is pretty galling for women, because, after all, men need women precisely because they are experts in the field of emotions, generally better than men at loving and caring. And in order to be good at loving and caring, women have to put right things that are wrong. By refusing to acknowledge that an emotional problem exists, men are undermining the caring they want and expect from their partners, sabotaging the fundamental work that needs to be done to keep their relationships alive.

How men 'win' arguments and break down relationships

When confronted with an emotional problem, the male strategy is commonly to remain impassive, to form a brick wall of ignorance and denial. 'I don't know what you're talking about. I don't understand what you mean. What you're saying is nonsense.' Blocking communication is a way of asserting superiority. To withdraw from involvement and withhold your opinion creates insecurity and disorientation in the person who wants access to your thoughts and feelings. Insecurity and disorientation lead to frustration, then rage.

Faced with a brick wall of denial, women react quite naturally by shouting, screaming and crying to try to break down the wall and reach the feelings of the man behind it. And when they lose their tempers and their heads, men can have the satisfaction of saying: 'Typical woman: overreacting and hysterical.' They don't take into account that it was their stonewalling that caused the anger to erupt in the first place.

The language we use is imbued with sexist attitudes that proclaim women's inferior status in society. Men apply certain words to female behaviour to put them down: these words are now used almost exclusively to describe women. Words such as 'demanding', 'complaining', 'nagging', 'overemotional', 'overreacting', 'irrational', 'clinging', 'insecure' and 'oversensitive' are labels applied by men without any consideration of the fact that they themselves provoke the female behaviour they are deploring.

The Ancient Greeks are responsible for that most offensively applied adjective, 'hysterical'. It derives from the Greek word for womb: when women in Ancient Greece lost their tempers, the men at the receiving end outrageously diagnosed 'a disorder of the womb'!

Men pride themselves on their cool-headed rationality, yet they do not tend to exercise reasonableness in discussions with women about emotional issues, which are after all crucial to their wellbeing. It would be unthinkable for a man in a work situation, when approached with a problem by a male colleague, to deny that that problem existed. Yet this is what happens time and time again in the domestic environment.

By cutting themselves off and acting superior, men may reduce their partners to incoherent rage and come out of the argument the unruffled 'winners', but each time they do so they deny responsibility for the relationship, and the relationship is the ultimate loser. Women get ground down by male 'superiority' to the point where they either stop participating, or get out. (Ninety per cent of the huge number of divorces that go through each year in the United States are initiated by women.)

Good relationships are based on equality. They are a dialogue between equals in which each opens heart and mind to the other. This is not possible if men refuse to listen to women and share responsibility for emotional problems.

HOW PRODUCTIVE ARGUING CAN STRENGTHEN A RELATIONSHIP

Conflict between two people can be dealt with in a number of ways: both parties can ignore it and stew; one party can refuse to be drawn, driving the other to screaming; each can fight to destroy the other in a slanging match; or the goal can be to convince the other person that you're right while listening to his point of view. Only the last form of argument is productive, because only this one is likely to end in agreement.

A good argument is creative because it involves both parties airing their opinions at full tilt and thrashing them out to reach a resolution, a new area of understanding. A slanging match leaves both parties frustrated, isolated and depressed, but productive arguing can be a very satisfying activity: it exercises the mind like a game of squash exercises the body. After a good argument the participants feel envigorated and restored. Productive arguing keeps a couple powerfully in touch with each other's thoughts and feelings.

In healthy arguing there's a feeling of forging ahead, of developing your own ideas on the run, and strengthening or modifying them as a reaction to those put forward by your partner. It's a risky business because you're breaking new ground, colonizing fresh territory where an agreement has not already been established. It can be frightening as well as exhilarating: there is always the possibility that your views may remain poles apart. But all creative ventures are leaps into the unknown, and all involve unpredictability and the risk of failure. Being creative is sticking your neck out and making a personal declaration, it's intensifying your feeling of self. Of course this makes you vulnerable, but it also strengthens you by defining your personality more clearly. Stating your case with passionate conviction brings you sharply into focus in your partner's eyes, and seeing you more clearly opens the way for understanding and eventual agreement. A fierce argument can often be moving and even sexually arousing: it is another way of experiencing your own and your partner's passion, and can often lead to passion in bed.

Conflict

HEALTHY VS. DESTRUCTIVE ARGUING

How do you tell the difference between healthy and destructive arguing? If you both feel stronger afterwards, and you have reached agreement, or at least partial agreement on some points, and you appreciate each other more, it was a healthy argument. If you feel worse: depressed, isolated, frustrated, coerced or rejected, and your relationship has diminished in stature, it was obviously a bad experience.

YES

- *Stick to the point*
- *Concentrate on getting your message across as clearly as you can*
- *Listen closely to what your partner has to say*
- *Question him/her to make sure you have understood exactly what he/she means*
- *Respect his/her point of view if you can*
- *Put your whole being into what you believe*
- *Speak with the passion you feel*
- *If you feel angry, be angry*
- *If you want to cry and shout, cry and shout*
- *If you see the opportunity for some common understanding, grab it and work on it*
- *Enjoy the adrenalin in yourself and your partner*
- *Allow yourself to laugh if it suddenly seems absurd*
- *If you are overwhelmed by love and admiration for your partner during the argument, tell him/her so*
- *Apologise with good grace if you were wrong*
- *Accept apologies generously*

NO

- *Don't beg, plead or whine: be strong*
- *Don't go over the same point: if your needle gets stuck, take a step backwards and start again from a broader viewpoint*
- *Don't get bogged down by bringing up old wounds*
- *Avoid personal insults: they are harmful and detract from the point you are trying to make*
- *Don't let yourself be dragged down into hurling abuse and name-calling: this will put the whole situation into reverse*
- *Don't try and win for the sake of it*
- *Don't use sex to try and patch up a fight that's unresolved: it will be premature and empty*
- *Don't resort to physical violence*
- *Don't walk out on an argument before it's finished*
- *Don't get bogged down in apportioning blame or picking holes: stick to major issues*
- *Don't fall into a distinctive pattern of drinking and arguing: a drunken row never solved anything for anyone*

THE POSITIVE POWER OF ANGER

Florence Nightingale, caring for the wounded, the sick and the dying of the Crimean War under appalling conditions, was once asked what motivated her to do such difficult work. She answered immediately, and with one word: 'Rage'.

This perhaps surprising answer is a perfect illustration of the immense power of anger diverted to positive use. If anger is so potent that it can run a hospital, then clearly the consequences of bottling it up inside the human mind and body are disastrous, and indeed researchers into cancer and other types of immune deficiency disease now believe that the suppression of powerful emotions is one of the prime causes of serious illness.

Self-help books often advise channelling anger into energetic activity, such as digging the garden or scrubbing the carpet, or letting off steam less productively by punching a pillow or smashing unwanted crockery. These activities may release harmful tension, but they do nothing towards sorting out what made you angry in the first place: you may end up physically exhausted, but the knotty problem remains unresolved.

The best way of coping with anger is to release it as soon as you feel it, to vent it not on the china cupboard, but where it belongs. If your partner makes you angry, then you are entitled to be angry with him or her. Women aren't usually as ready as men are to blow their tops, having been brought up in the belief that anger is 'unfeminine', but you will never thoroughly know yourself until you have experienced the full range of your feelings.

The idea of expressing raw emotion to your partner may be terrifying: what if he can't handle it and rejects you? The alternative is to play sweet tunes when you're feeling like thunder. Admittedly, if you aren't used to letting go, the explosion of feeling may be shocking to both of you, but it will also be a revelation. You will discover the force of your own emotions, and that you can express what you feel without losing your partner's love; and your partner will discover the limits of your tolerance. Being angry is a way of staking your emotional territory: it lets you both know exactly where you stand. Justified anger always commands respect.

However, many potentially explosive situations between you and your partner can be defused by dealing assertively with minor irritations as they occur, before anger is reached. Being assertive is not the same as being aggressive. It is letting your partner know what your needs are without fuss. If you fail to assert yourself and always tolerate impositions and absorb everything that grates on your nerves, you will find yourself constantly taken advantage of. Look inside yourself and find out what your needs are, then make them clear. In the mutual understanding that ensues, there will be no room for confusion. On the contrary, your positive, coping behaviour should inspire calm and confidence.

infidelity

Three quarters of all married people are, have been, or will be, unfaithful to their partners.

Paradoxically, today's more liberal attitude towards sexuality has strengthened our belief that once committed, whether legally married or not, partners should practise sexual exclusivity. This is the vow that distinguishes the life partnership from other more casual relationships. The desire to give this vow public importance is the reason that marriage is not declining in popularity, despite the realization that two in three end in divorce. Marriage shows the world that although there may have been other relationships, this is the one for whom the couple are prepared to 'forsake all others'.

Despite the best intentions, the ideal of sexual exclusivity is fulfilled in only a minority of marriages, and an astonishing seven out of ten partnerships succumb at one time or another to infidelity. How and why does this happen? What is it like to have an illicit affair? What do you feel, and how do you handle your feelings, when you discover your partner has been unfaithful? How is it possible to cope with jealousy? And what can be done to ensure that your partnership is one of the 30 per cent that remain intact?

So why do people have affairs?

The obvious answer is that people have affairs because something is missing in their prime relationship, which they either search for or suddenly find offered elsewhere. Boredom often creates its own opportunities.

Sex may be routine and uninspiring at home, but the potential for passion never dies, it just slumbers. Suddenly awakened, perhaps during a brief separation, the desire for more exciting sex can be the trigger for an impulsive fling. However, it seems that men and women who engage in long-term affairs are initially more strongly attracted, not by the desire for sex but by the possibility of increased intimacy. If a partnership has been allowed to grow stale and dull, with communication reduced to familiar basics, then it is possible for someone to come along whose lively and sympathetic interest will engage the attention,

Infidelity

kindle the affection, and eventually brim over into sexuality. An affair that provides a combination of intimacy and good sex comes close to the ideal relationship and can pose a serious threat to the established partnership.

Other people instigate affairs to prove their strength in a power struggle with their partner. Sometimes a man or woman newly committed to a relationship may panic, fearing a loss of independence, and have a brief affair to prove that they have not been completely 'taken over' by their partner. Another common move in the power game is to have an affair in retaliation, after you've found out that your partner has been unfaithful. In both cases the affair partner is chosen primarily for his or her usefulness rather than for any intrinsic appeal. However, what seems simply a strategic flexing of the muscles to the one who's indulging in it can often have unexpectedly serious repercussions.

The first two years of commitment, when both partners are settling down to sexual exclusivity, can be a vulnerable time, especially if one or both feel pressured into their new roles. Other times of transition to a new phase of the relationship may also see partners moving at a different pace, and therefore temporarily out of touch with each other. Pregnancy and childbirth bring some couples closer together and force others into separate private worlds. A man who feels excluded from his partner's love and attention by a new baby may seek affection elsewhere; a woman who has given up her job to look after home and family while her husband streaks ahead in his career may crave excitement and company from another man. When domestic circumstances change again and the woman returns to work after years of childrearing, the boost to her self-confidence may also lead her to accept attention from someone new.

THE 'UP'-SIDE OF AFFAIRS

An affair enters a dull life with the blaze of a comet, providing an intensity of attention that has been missing at home. It is an enormous boost to the ego to suddenly find yourself the cause of fascination, to rediscover your capacity for passion. And the whole package is exclusively and absolutely yours: it's the one thing you don't share with your partner. Of necessity it's wrapped in secrecy, and that intensifies the thrill. Indeed, the thrill of secrecy gives an affair a lift all of its own. Why should this be?

In our society we are brought up with the idea that sex should be kept hidden. Associated with our earliest sexual experiments are feelings of danger, excitement and shame. In an open adult relationship there is a different cocktail of sexual ingredients. While the partners are still new to each other there may be shyness and fear of the unknown, or fear of losing control, but once inhibitions have dissolved, there is nothing to hide. There is nothing forbidden, nothing to be ashamed about. If, in time, there is nothing to get excited about either, then the original potent mix of danger, excitement and shame can strike a powerful chord. These are three key ingredients of an affair, and they originate in deception. Where once we feared our parents would find out about our secret sex lives, now we hide our secret from our partners.

For some people, the challenge of outwitting their partner carries its own special reward. It may generate an enormous pleasure plotting your day so your partner won't see that black hole in the afternoon, which you intend to devote to your lover. Advance planning holds all the delight of anticipation. But afterwards, there's the tricky business of building an alibi.

It can help you to justify having an affair to yourself, if you can take pride in the lengths you go to to conceal it. You can kid yourself that you're being a good spouse: 'What she doesn't know won't hurt her.' Duping your partner so thoroughly has the double bonus of making you feel powerful, and making you feel tender, because your partner seems so innocent, so easily deceived. Paradoxically, your need to care for this vulnerable person you have under your control may increase: your affair may make you extra nice and attentive to your partner.

Of course, your happiness with your affair can also rub off on the rest of your life. If it provides you with what is missing at home, your satisfaction should brim over into your home life. You will be more tolerant, forgiving and generous, easier to live with. Your generosity will also be informed by guilt, and your desire to 'make up to' your partner for what she or he is unconsciously giving you. Many people who have affairs claim that it makes them better husbands or wives, because they stop demanding what their partners can't supply: they are secretly getting the missing ingredient from elsewhere, without rocking the boat. Some even go so far as to say that having affairs is the only thing that keeps their marriage together: the supreme justification for having your cake and eating it.

At the heart of the affair is the time you spend with your lover. The careful plans you have laid in order to meet, the secret location, the limited time at your disposal, all are geared to intensify the urgency of your feelings. Because this is truly private time, shut away from the rest of the world, you expect, and are able to get, the concentrated best from each other.

At the beginning of the affair at least, your lover is your 100 per cent ally, your best friend, your supremely understanding confidante. Disengaged for a few hours from reality, you can bask in each other's absolute attention. The secret capsule-like environment in which you meet enables you to achieve a closeness that would not be viable, or even desirable, in a free relationship.

THE 'DOWN SIDE' OF AFFAIRS

Probably the biggest disadvantage to having an affair is the guilt that it engenders. Since partnerships for life are founded on a vow of sexual exclusivity, having an affair means betraying your partner in the most fundamental way.

Togetherness

Infidelity

Your relationship was supposed to be honest and open, and now it is anything but. Affairs drive a wedge of deception between partners. Communication, which was probably at a low ebb anyway, can now never be fully restored. Time, emotional energy, and perhaps material benefits are stolen from the prime relationship, and maybe also from other areas of life. The more pleasure and deep satisfaction you get from your affair, the bigger the risk to your future, and the more worried you are likely to become.

It may be that you spent months agonizing over the decision, analysing what was wrong between you and your partner, trying to put things right, living the guilt before you technically even earned it. Or perhaps you leapt into your lover's bed without a second thought, then suffered terrible remorse once you found yourself becoming emotionally involved. Guilt is the widening gap between you and your partner, and you feel it every time you recognize the discrepancy between appearance and reality, between what you say and what you do.

Very few people enjoy lying, and building up a false picture of your life over a long period, and to someone who knows you and your routine very well, is a tricky business. One lie under scrutiny often necessitates the invention of a whole raft of lies that might suddenly spring a leak. Lying may be essential from time to time, but aspects of the truth are less uncomfortable to live with. Most people are bad at lying, and most partners have built-in lie detectors.

Living with guilt is not comfortable. It doesn't allow you to relax, or you might let out the secret; it no longer allows you to be fully yourself at home, where you should be able to relax. It means you must fragment your life, and keep the different parts of it carefully separate. Secretly redefining the original contract you made with your partner is a betrayal that pushes you further apart and adds another layer of guilt from which it is difficult ever to recover.

Closely allied with guilt is shame. But whereas guilt is private persecution, shame is what you feel when you are found out. The revelation of infidelity is always a shock, because the realization that you have been deceived never ceases to shock.

If both affair partners are married, there is a balance; each has a responsibility to another partner and another home life. Extra problems are created when a married person has an affair with a single person, because, if their relationship deepens, the single person may be less understanding of the married person's commitments and put more pressure on him or her to leave home. This situation can cause a heartache of indecision and can also be very disruptive to both relationships, especially, of course, if your lover decides to confront your partner.

There may be a point at which the guilt becomes unbearable, and this often happens when you start feeling guilty towards your lover as well as your partner. If the desire to rid your life of the complications of guilt is irresistible, you will have to end one or both of your relationships, and face the pain and mess that the decision will entail.

DO MEN AND WOMEN HANDLE AFFAIRS DIFFERENTLY?

In their book *Sexual Arrangements*, psychologists Janet Reibstein and Martin Richards argue that men and women do handle affairs differently. In the course of their research, they found that men having affairs tended to be able to adopt a segmented view of their lives, and devote separate blocks of time to the affair, to their home life and to their work.

Although the men they interviewed were not without guilt, they found it easier than women did to leave one aspect of their life behind when they moved into another. Men also tended to assume that their affair partners led similarly segmented lives. Because on the whole they did not discuss the 'rules' of the affair at the outset, again assuming their lovers were playing by the same book as them, they were often completely taken aback when the affair moved into a demanding emotional phase.

By contrast, women were careful to spell out the parameters of the affair before it started, making it quite clear just what their lovers could and could not expect. Women were less able to compartmentalize their feelings, and were constantly concerned about the effect their affair was having on their marriage, and vice versa. Because they were not able to separate the two sides of their life and divide their conscience, they felt

Infidelity

more guilt. Of course, women also tend to feel more guilt because of the double standard, which measures any show of male sexuality with tacit admiration and looks on female sexuality with disapproval. Women are supposed to be angels; men are allowed to be rogues.

Reibstein and Richards trace the different approach men and women have to their affairs back to their upbringing. Most of us, they say, were brought up by our mothers, or by female child minders or teachers. They argue that female carers empathize with their female charges, which encourages girls to relate closely to and identify with others; and that female carers treat their male charges as different and separate, which encourages boys to grow up learning how to cut off from those around them, to stand apart, and to be independent.

The end of the affair

The dynamic structure of an affair is different from that of a free relationship. It is based on extremes. In an affair, involvement and independence, togetherness and being apart, don't mingle to form a harmonious whole. Instead, they act on each other dramatically like the poles of a magnet. When affair partners are together, urgency requires that they let down all their barriers, give up all independence and merge their identities into one; and when they are apart, secrecy demands that they deny each other's existence. People in an affair alternate between total affirmation, and total suppression and denial. It's like rushing out of a steam bath and throwing yourself headlong into the snow.

The constant tension between the two extremes is bound to be unsatisfactory over time. The absolute togetherness may start to seem too much, or the absolute absence may feel too little. The artificiality of the situation begins to chafe. But if the boundaries are crossed, and messages and signals start to get through during absence, or attention and devotion waver below the 100 per cent mark during togetherness, the affair moves either towards replacing the prime relationship, or towards burning itself out.

Exposure and its aftermath

By no means all affairs end in exposure, but exposure is the official way in which your partner gets to find out about your affair. She or he may have known about it all along, or strongly sensed it and decided to keep quiet. Clues – slips of memory on your part, itemized telephone or credit card bills, stray notes or tickets, even little clues like drink unexpectedly on your breath or minute shifts of expression at certain points in a conversation – add up over time to create suspicion, then certainty. However, your partner may take a gamble on the fact that the affair won't usurp your marriage and decide to ride it out. Or she or he may be too insecure to risk confronting you. Only exposure will make you face the facts.

The only prediction that can be made with any confidence about the results of exposing an affair is that they are almost always totally unpredictable. Guilt over an affair can lead you to confess in an attempt to clear the slate, justify and explain yourself, and get sympathy and understanding. Don't kid yourself: sympathy and understanding are usually the last emotions that will be forthcoming from your partner. The revelation of infidelity, whether it comes from you or a third party, will pull the whole basis of your shared lives out from under your partner's feet like a rug. It will unleash jealousy and rage, and you will have to deal with devastating injury and crippling insecurity. Whether your partner leaves you or stays, your lives will be in turmoil for some time, and your relationship may never recover.

If you are the partner who has been betrayed, you will be feeling intolerably hurt. The rawness of your emotions and your bitterness at what you feel to have been wasted weeks, months or years, can combine with an overwhelming sense of rejection to produce feelings of utter worthlessness. If you believe you have nothing left to lose, you may find yourself acting with demeaning destructiveness or vindictiveness. Beware that if you try to make a public spectacle of your partner's lover, the person you will be doing the most damage to is yourself. Read the chapter on jealousy on page 84. Remember that you have done nothing wrong: your integrity is intact. Hang on to your dignity, and give full vent to your anger. Then give yourself time in which to consider your needs, and how best to meet them. You do have a choice, and you are in control. Put yourself first. If you decide to stay, make sure you renegotiate the terms of your relationship to your satisfaction.

WHY MOST AFFAIRS STAND LITTLE CHANCE OF BECOMING PERMANENT PARTNERSHIPS

Of course some people who have affairs do end up getting divorced from their partners and married to each other, and many affairs wreck marriages because of the pain they cause and the flaws they expose in the relationship. But most affairs, because of their very nature, don't make the transition to free partnerships.

People start affairs because there is some life spark lacking in their relationship at home. Affairs are designed to provide nothing but that missing spark. The spark is vital to an exciting and fulfilling life, but it is only one element. The prime relationship usually goes on providing the other elements: companionship, familiarity, security, family, friends, work and holidays all continue to be rooted at home. So the need for compatibility with the affair partner is specific and very limited. A couple who have chosen each other for sex and intimacy may get on like a house on fire in bed and in conversation, but if they were suddenly planted in a social or domestic setting, they could find themselves totally at odds. And this would be enough to kill the spark.

Then there is the unreality factor. Secret affairs thrive only in a vacuum outside the everyday world. Their intensity is due in part to the fact that they are forbidden. Making an affair public robs it of its hothouse magic and destroys its dynamism. An affair has to go through a change in order to survive in the real world. Lovers are used to enjoying each other's company and adoring attention for short periods of time, but the real world is a never-ending flow full of intrusions and distractions. Practicalities have to be faced. And domestic bliss is not likely to be high on the agenda if one or both parties are going through a painful divorce. Lovers who are used to seeing each other at their best now have to cope with guilt, and emotional and probably financial turmoil.

Once an affair is exposed, the chances of it surviving are drastically reduced. The focus shifts from the affair to the marriage, which has been ticking along quietly in the background, and now suddenly explodes. If the partners were out of touch before, they are now in touch again with a vengeance, while all the excitement of the affair is extinguished by guilt. Affairs of the sort designed to add spice to a dull life are now redundant, and even those that eventually become permanent partnerships take a precarious back seat while the partners sort through the rubble of their lives.

RETHINKING YOUR CONTRACT
Couples who stay together need to rethink the terms of their relationship. Does the affair mean that sexual fidelity is not possible, or that you are willing to give it another try? Will the betrayed partner ever be free of suspicion? Or will you decide now to experiment with open marriage, in which both of you are allowed other sexual relationships?

There was a vogue for open marriage in the '70s, when groups of people got together to form communes that espoused 'free love'. The communes were based on the idea that people are not property and, therfore, cannot be expected to tie themselves for life to one partner. It was argued that if couples promised to rid themselves of possessiveness and were open about their attachments to other men and women, a new ideal of love would be achieved. However, many of the communes disbanded, the relationships within them broken up by jealousy and guilt.

The fact is that it's very difficult to remain in a balanced partnership if you're having sex with other people. How do you keep it equal? Do you measure sexual involvement by frequency, turnover or intensity? And if you are absorbed elsewhere, how can you give your partner prime attention? The rules you make for an open marriage have to be clear and painstakingly drawn up. Some partners specify when and for how long they will allow each other to be with lovers; some specify where; some say: 'bed and sex only; no outings, no socializing together.' Will a complicated set of rules safeguard you from jealousy? Will sticking to it make you feel free?

A variation of open marriage is 'swinging and swapping', in which couples exchange partners, either within a group or within a foursome, and have sex, often

Infidelity

within each other's presence. Some couples try this in an attempt to provide sexual variety while remaining in strict control. The health risk aside, there are serious emotional risks involved in partner-swapping. If sex between you is not good, it can be very damaging witnessing your partner apparently enjoying sex with someone else. And if one of the partners is reluctant, and has agreed to join in only to please the other, it can be a sordid and degrading experience.

The best and safest way to revitalize your relationship is to concentrate exclusively on each other, to go away together if appropriate, to get to know each other again, and to find out the particular needs each of you has. In weathering the painful business of analysing what was missing in your relationship, you will find out how far you have to stretch yourself to meet those needs. The very fact that you have decided to try can go a long way towards healing the hurt.

not allowed to do anything that involves paying attention to people of the opposite sex. This is the attitude of a slave driver. Slaves are expected to function purely for their masters' service, convenience and pleasure, and jealous people want partners who toe the line and can account for their every action. 'What time did you leave work? Why are you so late home? Who was that you were talking to on the phone?' Jealous people deny the individuality of their partners. They are not supposed to exist except as partners.

Because of the inordinate demands they make, jealous people appear to be very strong and self-confident. If they suspect cause for jealousy, they will hammer away at it tooth and nail, until the 'truth' comes out. They will insist that harmless coincidences are lapses full of significance and add up to a betrayal. However minor the suspected betrayal, the jealous person will feel jusified in acting with hurt and indignation.

Behind this aggressive egotistical behaviour lurks the dreadful insecurity caused by an inferiority complex. Only if you feel unsure of your own worth will you be ready to believe that your partner is always looking for an opportunity to betray you. You imagine that you are undesirable, but that your partner is so phenomenally exciting to the other sex that seduction is bound to happen the second your back is turned. Haven't you got things a little out of perspective? Your partner chose you, and he didn't choose you because you were dull and he'd rather be with almost anyone else.

If you have such a low opinion of yourself and no confidence, you look to other people for approval, and measure yourself by what you see in their eyes. Because you feel so empty, you are desperate for their love, and fearful of losing it. Rejection, to you, is the ultimate disaster, and you are always on the lookout for signs that it might be coming your way. You behave like a child who sees nothing but black and white and screams the moment her mother leaves the room, fearing that she has been abandoned.

This behaviour is not likely to endear your partner to you: quite the reverse. But the jealous person, the person who feels herself to be intrinsically worthless and unloveable, is out to prove that she is right. She will go to any lengths to do so, including goading her partner about his attraction towards other women to the point where he begins to get interested in this as an option. When your husband stops loving you because you are a jealous nag, there is a perverse sense of satisfaction. You knew all along that this would happen, and you feel justified in saying you told him so. What you don't understand is that you brought it all upon yourself. This is a classic behaviour pattern of insecure people. Fearing rejection, they go out of their way to make sure they get it. It's the only way they feel they can stay in control.

UNLEARNING JEALOUSY

Babies and small children cry when their mother leaves the room because their life depends on her presence, and her absence feels like the end of the world. One of the important lessons of the early years is to recognize that absence is not terminal: the mother will come back; the child will survive. In the adult world, experience teaches us that the person we want most may not always come back. Rejection is a fact of life. But although rejection is painful, it is not a matter of life or death. We survive disagreements. We may even be strengthened by arguments resolved. If it comes to separation, we still survive.

● *THE FIRST STEP* towards unlearning jealousy is to realize that your survival does not depend on your partner. Yes, of course he is unique and irreplaceable as a person, but he is not irreplaceable as a partner. And your existence does not depend on whether or not he loves you. There is no need to behave as though he has the power to turn off your life-support machine. You and you alone have the power of nourishing yourself by investing belief in your enduring worth.

● *THE SECOND STEP* towards unlearning jealousy is to start believing in your enduring worth. Because they so lack confidence in their own worth, jealous people always believe that the hub of the universe is elsewhere. If you see your partner talking to another woman, you instantly assume that their conversation is more interesting than any you might have with him. You imagine he must find the other woman more beautiful and fascinating than he finds you. Instantly, you perceive your partner as polarized on this paragon of desirability, while you yourself pale into emptiness. Don't be so quick to devalue yourself. How could you have become less just because someone else has walked into the room? The hub of your universe lies within you, and it will continue to do so all your life. Your life force is what your partner relates to. The dynamics of your relationship are between the two of you, and in your power as much as his.

● *THE THIRD STEP* is to be aware of your power. The jealous person presents herself as a victim of her partner's bad behaviour. The status of victim is demeaning. It says: 'I am not in control of my life; someone else is. I have no power to act; I let things be done to me.' This is nonsense: we all have the power to act. You need to break the cycle and take control. Instead of mutely accepting that you are dependent on your partner's approval, concentrate on the power of approval you have within you to give him. Instead of acting negatively, nagging and complaining, try acting positively, by letting your partner know in what ways and how much you appreciate him. Reinforcing the positive aspects of your relationship will do both of you the power of good. If you are no longer attacking him, worrying him with your suspicions, he can let down his defences and start enjoying your company again. And you will feel good because you have relaxed the tension and taken the power of approval into your own hands.

Togetherness

▪ THE FOURTH STEP is to take equal responsibility for your relationship. When you start thinking of yourself as whole and powerful, you will feel the need to cling gradually slipping away. When you begin to see yourself as not inferior but equal, you can stop acting as your partner's keeper. When you realize you have the power to give, you will start to feel generous. Now you can give your partner the freedom your jealousy was denying him. You will be able to allow him to enjoy socializing with other people, secure in the knowledge that this will not affect the way he feels about you or threaten your relationship. And by centring your power within yourself and standing apart from him, you will have given him the freedom to come to you.

LIVING WITH A JEALOUS PARTNER

Jealousy in another person is extremely difficult to live with, because jealous people always blame you for their unhappiness. Unless of course you are being unfaithful or behaving provocatively, you must make it clear that you are not the cause of your partner's misery, and that jealousy is a self-induced condition for which he alone is responsible.

A jealous partner will bombard you with constant detailed questions concerning your whereabouts and your motives, and the suspicious scrutiny of your life will be hard to tolerate. You cannot possibly comply by giving all the answers, as there would never be time to do anything else: the more questions you answer, the more material you are supplying for his suspicions to take root in.

Try to train your partner out of the habit of grilling you about the time you spend away from him. Tell him that he will have to be satisfied with a simple answer, and stick to it. If he wants to push you further, remind him that repeatedly accusing you of something you have not done will eventually drive you away, not just emotionally but physically. Show him that his behaviour is nothing short of emotional terrorism. Talk to him gently about his jealousy and offer to help him to do something about it. If he refuses to accept responsibility for the damage he is doing to your relationship, you may have no option but to try separation.

DO YOU HAVE A PROBLEM WITH JEALOUSY?

- ☐ *Do you keep track of your partner's every move?*
- ☐ *Do you question him closely when he deviates from his routine?*
- ☐ *Do you disapprove of him talking to/laughing with other women?*
- ☐ *Do you insist on knowing every last detail of his telephone and other conversations?*
- ☐ *Do you cross-question him, in the belief that you will catch him out deceiving you?*
- ☐ *Do you nag and blame?*
- ☐ *Do you depend on his approval?*
- ☐ *Do you live by the same set of rules, or do you have rights and privileges that your partner is not allowed?*
- ☐ *Do you believe that women are constantly trying to seduce him?*
- ☐ *Do you resent time that he spends away from you?*
- ☐ *Do you have tantrums when you don't get your own way?*
- ☐ *Do you believe your partner has no right to stop loving you?*
- ☐ *Do you believe you are worthless if your partner stops loving you?*

If you answer yes to any of these questions, you are jealous to a degree that may bother your partner. Get your partner to answer the questions too, then answer them for each other ('Does he keep track of my every move?' etc.) and compare results. If there is a problem, talking about it is the first step towards putting it right.

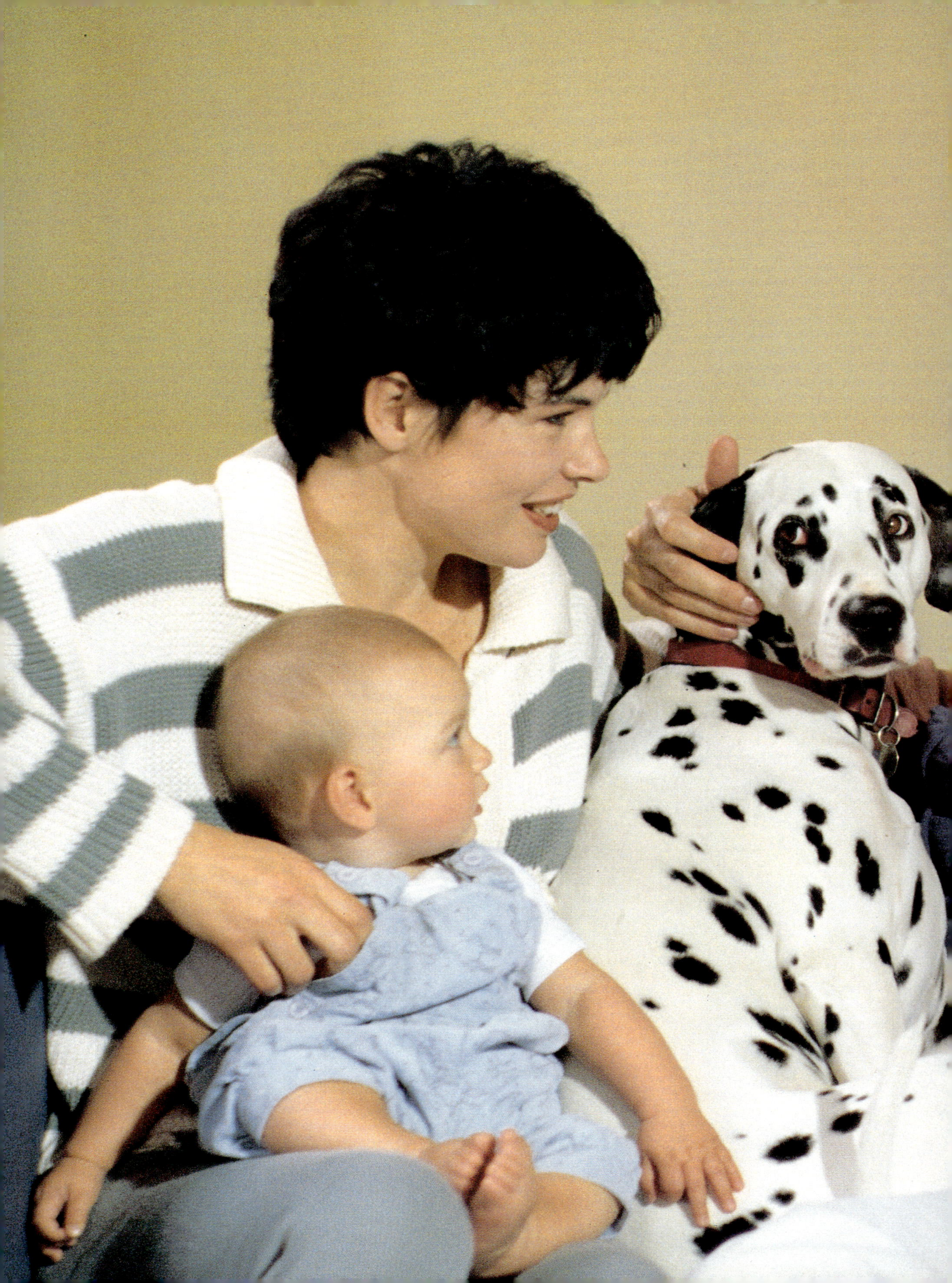

family life

from couple to family

The majority of couples who are committed to long-term relationships become parents; there is a feeling that having a family makes them complete and fulfilled.

In the privileged countries of the West people no longer have children out of economic necessity or to provide for their old age, but out of a desire to experience a different kind of love and companionship. They look forward to caring, being responsible, growing up, and linking into a family network that gives them permanence and continuity. Through their children they hope to learn more about themselves and each other, and thereby find a new understanding of their own parents.

But all the surveys produced on the subject show that having children brings stress as well as happiness. Initially there are great physical demands on new parents: feeding, changing and washing babies seem to take practically 24 hours a day, causing loss of sleep and exhaustion. It is emotionally draining to feel you can't cope and to see the responsibility of looking after your child stretching out across the years ahead. Being a parent also puts pressure on your relationship in different ways.

There may be financial difficulties if one partner gives up work. And giving up a job is not just giving up money, it's losing independence. The partner who stays at home is usually the woman, and many women are torn between the desire to look after their baby and the freedom to pursue a satisfying career. Although they love the idea of being close to the baby and watching her develop, they miss the adrenalin, the companionship and the challenge of their work environment, and may feel loneliness and resentment. Being dependent on her partner's income may sometimes make a woman feel secure and protected, but it can also sometimes have a debilitating effect.

From couple to family

Both partners lose freedom as their lives focus on the baby. However hard you try not to let it happen, your social life is bound to be disrupted by the demands of the new arrival to be fed, changed and comforted. Friendships with people who are not parents may lapse for a while, at least until the baby ceases to completely dominate conversation, but friendships with other new parents will grow.

The feeling that your baby is now the number one priority in your lives can force your partner into second place: it's quite common for new fathers to feel excluded and neglected, and this causes hurt and resentment.

Early parenthood is a time of radical change, when the sheer burden of work makes it inevitable that domestic roles become more clearly demarcated. The result of this can be that partners lose sight of one another under the roles they adopt and let the stress of parenthood get in the way of intimacy. But if you are well prepared for the problems as well as the pleasures that having a baby entails, you can use this time of radical change to strengthen the bond between you and to grow, as individuals and as a couple. In growing, you will develop new resources and find new ways of supporting and caring for each other.

Helping each other cope, understanding the doubts and the difficulties that your partner is facing, and above all sharing in the love of your baby, can open new vistas of passion and tenderness in your relationship.

Sex and conception

Giving up contraception after you have decided to start a family often gives sex a new deeper meaning, and both partners may give themselves more fully in making love. Sharing a secret hope for the future brings the two of you closer in emotional and sexual fulfilment.

But if months pass and nothing happens, disappointment and anxiety can intrude on your intimacy. Sex can start to become a means to an end, rather than a spontaneous expression of your feelings. You are less likely to get pregnant if you are 'trying' so hard that you no longer enjoy making love for its own sake. If you sense that this is beginning to happen, hide the calendar and give up intercourse altogether for a while; just hold each other close and cuddle instead. It's important to take the pressure off and relax. You can't make love and mean it just because you've calculated that you should be ovulating on that day. Wait until you are both aroused, and make love because you want each other, not with the detached feeling that you are conducting a scientific experiment.

Infertility

Up to 10 per cent of couples who would like to have a baby are unable to conceive. In around 30 per cent of cases there are problems with both partners; the remainder are divided roughly equally between the sexes.

A major cause of infertility in women is scarring of the Fallopian tubes left by pelvic inflammatory disease (PID), which happens when the sexually transmitted diseases gonorrhoea or chlamydia are not treated quickly enough. The feeling that her own sexual behaviour may be responsible for her infertility can be devastating for a woman. Other causes of female infertility are blockages of the Fallopian tubes, hormonal irregularities that result in a failure to ovulate, and high acidity in the genital tract. Female fertility decreases sharply after the age of 40; male fertility declines more slowly, and at age 55 it is still three-quarters of what it was at age 25.

Causes of male infertility are low sperm count or low sperm motility, or poor sperm quality. Environmental pollution affects fertility in both sexes.

Treatments for infertility are improving all the time. In 5 per cent of cases, couples are able to conceive once shown how to time ovulation by taking the woman's temperature at various points in her menstrual cycle, and have been given advice on which positions are best for conception. Other treatments include drugs to correct hormone imbalance, surgery to remove blockages and douches to correct acidity. Couples may also consider in vitro (test tube) fertilization and semen donation.

Infertility often causes great unhappiness and severe damage to a relationship, because the knowledge that you are unable to conceive or to give your partner a baby can generate deep feelings of failure, guilt and blame, even if your powers of reasoning tell you it is no one's fault. If sex is not 'working' for you in the way you want, making love can seem pointless and empty, and a cold void can grow up between you.

If you are infertile you are likely to feel anger and resentment and view your partner's understanding and sympathy as condescension. A deep sense of failure and rejection could lead you into an affair to 'prove' your sexual potency in a different way. You may feel that your partner wants a child more than he or she wants you. The fear of being left for someone who could provide the wanted baby could – paradoxically – terrify you into behaviour that makes it impossible for your partner to stay. Forcing things in the direction you least want them to go in is a way of staying in control that comes instinctively to some people, but of course it does neither of you any good.

The important thing is to keep in touch with your feelings and not to repress your anger or your fears, or they may be thwarted into the damaging sort of behaviour described above. Keep the channels of communication between yourself and your partner open. Share your pain and disappointment, and your outrage at the unfairness of it all. Try to work through it together. It's not only a matter of coming to terms with infertility, but of realizing the love that you wanted to give to a baby of your own by expressing it in a different way, perhaps through other caring relationships, or through a special line of work. Shared grief can bring you and your partner closer together and help you find this new purpose in life.

Pregnancy and childbirth

The discovery that you are pregnant can trigger a whole range of conflicting emotions. Along with a great surge of happiness can come a sense of panic at the inevitability of the process that is now underway, and a feeling of being trapped within it.

However much you want the baby, you are bound to experience moments of doubt and fear. Will the pain of childbirth be intolerable? What will the advent of the baby do to your relationship? Will it dull your love in any way? Will your partner still find you attractive?

The father-to-be often has similar mixed feelings. On the one hand there is the exhilaration of having 'proved' his biological function, which gives an almost mystical feeling of belonging in the generations of the human race; but on the other is the thought of the tremendous emotional and financial responsibility that being a parent holds. Because the baby is growing in his partner's body and not in his own, a man may feel threatened by the closeness from which he is unavoidably excluded. If the pregnancy was unplanned, your partner might need to be reassured that you did not deliberately 'forget' to take the Pill.

Whatever your doubts or fears, you should talk about them. Use the nine months your baby needs to grow inside you, to grow yourselves into parents. You will need this time to make adjustments and plans, to 'make a nest' for your baby in your home and in your emotions.

Pregnancy and your relationship

The female body undergoes an enormous physical and hormonal upheaval during pregnancy, and although the source of the upheaval is very private, your body may quickly seem to have become public property. Doubtless parents and parents-in-law are overjoyed at the news, but as it spreads, you may get the feeling that you have been put 'on

Pregnancy and childbirth

Family life

show', and that some people are more interested in your pregnancy than they are in you. Use the fact that you tire easily and may often feel sick – at least in the first three months – to put off social engagements that don't really appeal, and retreat into privacy with your partner as much and as often as you like.

The medical examinations that you will be undergoing as you pass through the antenatal system can also give you the impression that your body has been taken over – this time by a team of experts. It's important not to give up responsibility for your pregnancy. The hospital, its doctors and technology are there to help, to provide a backup, but if you don't play an active part, by questioning and understanding what is going on, and by involving your partner as much as you can, you may lose the very personal sense of responsibility for the baby inside you.

So take your partner along to antenatal classes, buy a book on pregnancy and childbirth, read it together, and discuss what sort of birth you would like and what sort of parents you will want to be. Imagine the kind of things you will do together once you are a family. Now you know a baby is on the way, how do you feel about the plans you made for looking after her before you became pregnant? Do you still feel a childminder is the best option, or do you now long to give up work to care for the baby yourself? Would you be able to afford to lose one salary? How would you feel about giving up financial independence and your career? How does your partner feel about taking financial responsibility?

Discussing your future together can be both exciting and enriching. As you grow into parents, you will see qualities in each other that are only just now beginning to mature.

CHOOSING THE BIRTHPLACE: HOME OR HOSPITAL?

The main advantage of a hospital birth is obviously that expertise and technology are on hand to provide conditions of maximum safety for mother and baby. Your partner may feel particularly strongly that you should have the baby in hospital, because he may be terrified of the possibility of having to deliver it himself if you have it at home.

The main complaint people have against hospital deliveries is that they are too impersonal: that medical staff and machines take over too much, preventing the mother and her partner from sharing to the full what should be an intensely private and emotional experience. Many women object to the use of drugs, preferring to remain conscious even if it does mean experiencing a lot of pain, and believing that the chemicals may affect the baby. The bright lights and the medical routine seem alien, especially in the first few minutes after birth, when the new family needs privacy for bonding.

More and more women are opting to have their babies at home when they can. Home obviously offers comfort and familiarity, and the presence and support of your partner throughout. Some women

Pregnancy and childbirth

may also wish to have their children present at the birth, and this is not normally allowed in most hospitals.

Most first babies are born in hospital and there may be medical reasons why this is the best place for you to have your baby, but even if a home birth is out of the question, you should find out as early as possible during your pregnancy what sort of choices will be open to you, in both the type of hospital care, and the method of giving birth. Not all women feel comfortable with the idea of lying on their backs with their feet in stirrups: you may prefer to give birth standing or squatting, or even under water.

Underwater births can take place in an ordinary bath or in a special tank, big enough for the mother, her partner and the midwife to stand in. Being warm and buoyant, the water gives the mother comfort and support; the baby doesn't drown because she is still receiving oxygen through the umbilical cord. The mother gets out of the water and squats over a basin to deliver the placenta.

Hospitals offer several different delivery schemes, and there should be a choice in hospitals near you. To help you choose, arrange to visit the hospitals in your catchment area with your partner to familiarize yourselves with the sight of the equipment of the delivery ward before you go in to have your baby.

Family life

COMMON WORRIES FOR PARENTS AS BIRTH DRAWS NEAR

- PAIN Try to see the pain as productive, as helping you give birth to your baby, rather than as pain directed at you. Work with the pain instead of defending yourself against it. Your partner can help enormously by breathing with you, giving you physical and moral support and confidence and encouraging you to relax. Note also that there is no shame or defeat in accepting painkilling drugs if the pain becomes too much to bear. You don't have to tough it out.

- LOSS OF CONTROL The fact that your body will take over can feel frightening. You may be worried about your waters breaking, and about losing control of your bowels and bladder, not to mention your emotions. There is nothing to be ashamed about. Birth, like sex, is a natural expression of your body. You are not going to be judged, because there are no standards: this is a unique experience, and it's yours to live.

- LOSS OF INDIVIDUALITY If you are going to have the baby in hospital, you will both be anxious to avoid the feeling that you are just being processed through the system. This is why it's so important to visit the delivery ward and make personal contact with the staff before you are admitted. Don't give in to the feeling that the birth is being controlled by experts and machines: the close involvement of your partner will help you focus on yourself and your natural abilities.

THE FATHER-TO-BE

As the birth draws near, the woman's condition makes her the subject of much interest and concern. This can make her partner feel shut out at a time when he will be trying to cope with the extra responsibility that the baby will bring. With the birth of the baby, the focus of your relationship will change, and the man especially may feel a sense of loss when he remembers the spontaneity and freedom that you used to share.

Try not to see your man as just a help and a support. He will undoubtedly be this, but he also has needs of his own, and most important is the need to feel loved, wanted and understood, particularly when most of the love and understanding from friends and relatives will be centred on you and the baby.

Don't forget that you are having the baby together. If your partner can share your education into parenthood – by going to the antenatal clinic and attending childbirth classes – then you will both know how to handle, feed and bath your baby and there should be no need for you to appear to be in charge with him as the 'bumbling helper'.

There is nothing more alienating for a new father than to have his baby snatched from him by his partner because he is not handling her like she does. Sharing the experience of childbirth is the best way of ensuring that you both have a strong bond with the baby from the start. Men who are present at the birth say that it is an experience they would not have missed for the world.

THE FATHER'S ROLE DURING LABOUR

Research has shown that women who have the help and support of their partner (or a close friend) at the birth have a shorter labour, less need for painkilling drugs and feel generally happier about the experience than women who have only medical support. So the father's presence during labour has a very positive effect. But what does it involve? The father's role is to stay completely tuned in to his partner. He should concentrate entirely on her needs, and give her physical and moral support. Attending childbirth classes will be of great help in anticipating what the mother's needs might be.

1. Your first priority is to stay calm. Remember that the pain your partner is experiencing is productive: support her in going with the pain by breathing with her as you have both been taught, and by encouraging her.

2. Use positive and not negative instructions. For instance, instead of saying: 'Don't tense up', remind her to relax. Give her plenty of reassurance and praise.

3. Physical contact is very important. She may want you to massage her thighs if they get cold and shaky, and she will need you to hold her shoulders or arms firmly during contractions.

4. Give her your undivided attention. Don't get distracted by the machinery in the delivery room and don't get chatting with the staff. Just ask questions when you need to and make sure you understand what's going on, so that you can tell your partner how labour is progressing. And don't leave the delivery room unless you absolutely have to: you may be asked to leave, but if you really want to stay, usually you should be allowed to.

5. Contractions often stop for a while just before the birth. Your partner might like to be sponged down, or to take a shower, or to move about. Don't hurry her: the baby will come when she's ready; this is not a race against time.

6. In the final stage of labour, don't try to persuade your partner to take painkillers if she doesn't wish to. This should be her decision alone. Remember to tell her to 'open up' rather than to 'push'. When the baby comes, you or the midwife should 'catch' her and put her straight on to her mother's chest. This is a very intimate moment and medical staff will usually want to respect your privacy. You may be more overcome by emotion than you suspected was possible.

a baby in the house

Most parents are very excited to bring their new baby home for the first time. They experience delight and elation as they get to know their child by eye contact, feeding, rocking, and cuddling.

The advent of the baby will make major differences to your life, and during the first weeks of new parenthood, you will need to adjust to a new routine and to a new phase of your relationship with your partner.

SHARING RESPONSIBILITY FOR THE NEW ROUTINE
New fathers should take paternity leave if at all possible. It's much better that you share the first few weeks of your baby's life and establish a routine of caring for her together, than that one of your mothers moves in. The presence of a grandmother, who has 'done it all before', is bound to make you both feel incompetent, no matter how well-meaning she is. The presence of his mother-in-law could well make a man feel redundant and excluded from the care of his new baby. Use this time to build up your confidence and sense of togetherness by coping with the baby yourselves. The community midwife will visit daily for about 10 days, and the health visitor once every week or 10 days thereafter, for as long as you need her.

Until you are so used to it that you are able to do it automatically, the round of feeding and nappy-changing will dominate your lives. Keep housework to a minimum, and spend as much time as you can resting together while your baby sleeps. Think of it as going to ground to recuperate and gather your strength. As soon as you are feeling more vigorous, you can take it in turns to mind the baby so that your partner can get some free time. All the baby care can be shared except, of course, breastfeeding, but you can learn to express breast milk so that your partner can bottle feed the baby during the night.

When your baby is very small, you may want her cot or cradle next to your own bed so that you can feed her in the night without too much disruption. But

A baby in the house

as feeds get further apart you will probably decide to put her in her own room so that you don't wake every time she stirs.

THE 'BABY BLUES'

The reality of having a baby is bound not to be quite as you imagined it would be. New mothers sometimes suffer the 'baby blues': fits of weeping and depression. It is often difficult to understand why you feel unhappy, because there are several factors involved.

FIRST, although you have given birth to your baby, you have 'lost' the baby that you were carrying and nourishing within you for nine months. It comes as something of a shock when the real baby replaces the fantasy baby. It's like a rude awakening from a dream - and it leaves you with a feeling of bewilderment and emptiness.

SECOND, after all the anticipation and excitement and the intense drama of the birth, there could well be a feeling of let-down, that the party is over. This may be brought home especially when all the admiring visitors have gone and left you to struggle with your unfamiliar and demanding routine.

THIRD, there is the hormonal upset that your body has undergone and is still undergoing.

FOURTH, there is sheer exhaustion. It is important for partners to give each other a lot of emotional support at this time. The experience of childbirth releases powerful emotions in men too, and they are often torn between exhilaration and depression in the first few days.

SEX AFTER CHILDBIRTH

New parents often want to know how long it will be before they are able to resume their normal sex life. The answer is that it depends on how quickly the woman's body heals, and of course on how she feels about her sexuality.

Nowadays, episiotomy (a cut into the perineum – the tissue between the vagina and anus – to prevent laceration during childbirth) is no longer routinely performed, but even if you have not had one, you are likely to feel severely sore and uncomfortable for a time. If you have had an episiotomy, sex may be painful for quite a long time. Consult your doctor or health visitor; don't suffer in silence. The fact that your body has changed may take some coming to terms with. You will notice that your genitals are slightly softer and not so tight. You may have scar tissue that you or your partner may be aware of for months, or even years, afterwards. Your breasts will obviously be swollen and heavy and your womb will not have shrunk back to its former size. Exercise will help you get back in shape, and the midwife or physiotherapist will recommend some postnatal exercises. Pelvic floor exercises are particularly useful.

When you feel ready for intercourse, take it very gently. Ask your partner to use his fingers and a lubricating jelly first, and guide his hand so that you can show him what kind of caresses you can enjoy and which are still painful. Of course, if you have had a Caesarean this will not be a problem. Choose positions that are comfortable for you, such as side by side, and move very tentatively to begin with. Orgasm will exercise the muscles in your womb and help it get back into shape. Milk may spurt from your breasts when you come. Sex after childbirth can add a new dimension to your love for one another, because of the deepened physical knowledge and emotional bond that you share. (However, note that a crying baby has a dampening effect on passion!)

MATERNITY LEAVE

Maternity rights will be standardized across the European Community in 1994 when a new Directive on the Protection of Pregnant Women comes into force. This will give all working women the right to a minimum of 14 weeks' maternity leave. At present the British system of maternity rights is complex, and you should ask your employer or consult an expert body to discover your entitlement.

All pregnant women have the right to time off work to keep medical appointments and attend antenatal classes. If you are working with chemicals or X-rays or other potentially harmful processes, you have the right to be transferred to a different job or working area.

If, when you become pregnant, you have been in full-time employment with the same employer for two years, or part-time between eight and 16 hours a week for at least five years, you are entitled to 11 weeks' leave before the birth and 29 weeks' afterwards, with statutory maternity pay for 18 weeks. If you have been with your current employer for more than six months but less than two years, you qualify for a reduced rate of maternity pay. If you have only just joined your current employer and find yourself pregnant, you still qualify for state maternity allowance, which can be claimed from your local Department of Social Security for 18 weeks.

If in doubt, contact The Maternity Alliance, 15 Britannia Street, London WC1X 9JP, telephone 071 837 1265,

OR

The Working Mothers' Association, 77 Holloway Road, London N7 8JZ, telephone 071 700 5771.

If you are dismissed or made redundant because you have become pregnant, you can claim for sex discrimination or unfair dismissal at an industrial tribunal.

Contact the Equal Opportunities Commission, Overseas House, Quay Street, Manchester M3 3HN, telephone 061 833 9244 or any other equivalent organization for advice on how to proceed.

Children and your relationship

The advent of children inevitably changes your relationship: Some may find it fuses a deeper bond; others that it drives a wedge between them.

Daily Express readers provided the information in this chapter by responding to a questionnaire on how having children affects your relationship. The space available here cannot do justice to the insight their answers gave into marriage – the answers, in fact, form the basis of a future book.

What follows is a selection of answers, carefully chosen for its usefulness to potential parents.

Q. Describe your feelings when you found out you were pregnant.

A. Most mothers-to-be and their partners felt a bewildering mixture of acute feelings probably best summed up as elation spiked with fear. They described themselves as ecstatic, excited, apprehensive, nervous, shocked, proud. A minority of men felt despondent.

Q. How did the pregnancy affect your relationship?

A. Many said there was no change. For a considerable number of women, however, this was the beginning of a journey they felt they were making on their own. Some men were put off sex by pregnancy, and, in particular, did not like feeling the baby move while they were making love. Some women found their libido decreased during the final months, probably due to a subconscious fear of 'hurting the baby'. Some women mentioned getting round this problem with oral sex; some men wrote of the enjoyment of experimenting with new and more comfortable positions. One woman wrote that sex during pregnancy was the best ever, because she felt so utterly feminine.

Q. Describe your experience of childbirth. Was your partner present? How did he feel about the whole thing? Did it bring you very close, or did you feel you were going it alone?

A. Some couples agreed in advance not to share the experience, but among those who were together, there was an

Children and your relationship

Family life

overwhelming consensus of opinion that women benefitted enormously from their partner's presence and support; for men, it was the most emotional experience of their lives. Most couples felt very close. 'My partner was present throughout. He was incredulous about the whole thing. He hated the pain I was in – he was supportive – I felt we were very close. I certainly did not think I was alone.' 'He found it all mind-blowing. It was one of the most exciting and emotional times of our lives. He was very supportive and involved. He wept when the baby was born. I was moved by his obvious emotion.'

Q. What were the main pleasures and problems you experienced in the first few weeks of your baby's life?

A. A typical response was: 'The pleasure of caring for our new daughter and seeing her do things for the first time. A lack of sleep made us both irritable but we got through it.' For some women the problem was 'that my husband expected everything to carry on as before'. In a considerable number of cases, the father was unwilling or unable to adjust to changed circumstances or accept responsibility. One woman wrote: 'My partner went out more and more and when the baby cried, I felt helpless, isolated and very angry. Because I was alone so much in the evenings, it took enormous self-control not to harm the baby.'

Q. Did you stay at home to look after the baby? How did you cope with loss of independence?

A. Several women agreed with this very positive answer: 'I did stay at home, with both children. I hadn't lost my independence, I'd gained a new and important responsibility.' While most found great satisfaction in child rearing, many whose partners did not involve themselves with the baby expressed frustration. 'I felt I'd lost a lot of my identity as an individual.' 'I would never be just me again.' 'I felt mumsy. I wondered who I was.'

Q. How did being part of a family change you?

A. Here the rift in weaker marriages widened. Where both were not equally committed to family life, partners tended to drift apart: 'It seemed to me that over the years he became more interested in his work. I wasn't number one all the time. I lived in a haze of babies, while the world carried on without me.' Those who were committed to sharing their children grew stronger and closer: 'The whole experience made us grow up and accept that we had responsibilities. It gave some meaning and motivation to my husband in his career.'

Q. How has your sex life changed?

A. For most couples, lack of privacy, lack of time, and exhaustion have taken their toll. One man wrote: 'Not as frequent, as we have to be careful about where and when! We have learned to relax and be more adventurous (but quieter).' The solution of one couple is: 'Sex becomes something to enjoy when the kids are all out of the house on a Saturday afternoon.' Though many enjoy

For many, family life has pushed their sex life right into the background, for some even off the agenda altogether. 'There is little excitement and I often can't be bothered,' is the type of answer frequently given.

Q. What are the best things about sharing parenthood?

A. 'Enjoying the creation and development of a new human being who is part of each of you', was a sentiment expressed by most parents. Many mentioned laughter, love and the fun of playing together. However, a large number of women reacted angrily to this question and said that there was no sharing of parental responsibility with their partner: the upbringing of their children fell solely to them.

Q. What are the worst things about sharing parenthood?

A. Arguments about disciplining the children were the worst feature of many parents' lives, followed by arguments with the children, and then the problem of children trying to play one parent off against the other and to drive a wedge between them.

Q. What is the one thing that you have learned over the years that you feel could be useful to other couples thinking of embarking on family life?

A. The most frequent and strongly expressed piece of advice to prospective parents was to be sure that both partners are mature enough to be able to handle the responsibilities of family life. Very many women reported that their husbands could not cope at all and reverted to a bachelor lifestyle, playing squash or drinking every night of the week, while they were left to bring up their children single-handed. Divorced women with children were almost invariably happier with second partners who were enthusiastic about fatherhood.

Many advised prospective parents to discuss their ideas about upbringing and discipline before deciding to have a family, because of the years of conflict these issues often caused.

Some wise words were written on how to survive parenthood. One woman wrote: 'Our friendship is the cornerstone of our marriage. We have encouraged each other's interests and hobbies and allowed each other the time and space to be alone, if that is what is needed. I realized a long time ago that once the children were gone, I was going to be left with my husband, and if I didn't put that relationship before my relationship with my children, I was going to be left with nothing.'

Very many people stressed the need above all other things to keep talking to each other and to communicate your thoughts and feelings: 'It is very important not to forget that you are still identities in your own right, and not just mum and dad.'

Another woman summed it up like this: 'Try to always put each other first. Try not to take all your problems out on each other. Talk over everything, but don't forget to *listen* to what your partner says, and also to what he doesn't say. Learn to laugh together.'

the growing family

Having a family brings a whole complexity of demands on your time and attention. Through your child you become 'plugged in' to the community – whether you like it or not.

Even before the birth you are involved with your baby's health care, and you get to know other parents-to-be through the antenatal clinic. As your child grows you become involved with her education, and with the families you meet through her playgroup and school. You also reinforce your bonds with your own family and with that of your partner: grandparents in particular will want to play an active part in your child's upbringing.

Family and community life can be richly absorbing, but sometimes you may think back with nostalgia to the days when your time was free and you could make spontaneous decisions without having to consider the needs of others. Your family and its growing network of connections can consume so much of your time and energy that you have little or none left over for yourself or to share with your partner. The middle years of marriage also see growing financial pressure to make significant progress at work. The danger is that the heart of your relationship will suffer neglect.

TIME TO YOURSELVES

Considering yourselves as parents first and partners second certainly makes for a stable home life and a secure environment in which your children can grow up, but what of your responsibility towards each other? When you do have a moment to yourselves, what do you talk about? Do you tap into each other's feelings like you did when you first met? Do you ask personal questions and get personal answers? Or does all your conversation revolve around your children, home improvements, career moves and family holidays? Do you feel that the individuals you once were have become completely saturated in the roles of parent, partner, and householder?

Family life can drown out intimacy unless you work very hard to maintain a

The growing family

sense of your own and each other's individuality. A teething baby crying in the night, a small child who creeps in to share your bed, older children who get up early and stay up late: it's easy to see how partners come to regard themselves and each other as parents rather than as lovers and friends.

In order to stay lovers and friends, parents must keep time for themselves, right from the start. This means being firm about your right to privacy.

● *Don't allow small babies and toddlers to dominate your evenings: try to get them used to regular bedtimes. Make sure your children go to bed at the same time each evening, even if they don't go to sleep right away but lie in bed reading or playing quietly in their rooms. Explain to them that you all need private time in which to relax.*

● *As your children grow, teach them the value of privacy. This is best done by showing them the courtesies and consideration you wish for yourselves. If you want your bedroom to be your private zone, they will be more willing to respect your wishes if you treat them equally, by not walking into their rooms unannounced or rummaging through their personal belongings without permission.*

● *Giving teenagers time and space in which to pursue their own interests will make them more understanding of your need for some quiet while you read a book or listen to the radio.*

● *Make sure your own parents, on both sides, also respect your right to privacy. Sometimes it can be difficult keeping over-intrusive relations and in-laws at bay without hurting either their feelings or those of your partner, but unless you are pleasantly firm, they can take over. Agree with your partner on a joint approach – third parties have a habit of driving a wedge between partners who differ.*

The solution can be to try and put grandparents' energy and interest to positive use. Get them to look after their grand children, preferably in their own homes, so the two of you can have time to yourselves, and everyone will be happy. Don't let them spoil the children though; put your foot down about sweets and other treats: they should not undermine your authority with overindulgence.

● Neighbours can also pose a threat to your privacy, if you let them. As with parents and in-laws, neighbours who 'pop in' and then can't be got rid of, are liable to cause considerable tension between the partner who listens politely and the partner who is unable to hide frustration and resentment and takes noisy refuge in the other room.

Be aware of your partner's feelings and don't allow intruders, whether they are related to you or not, to spoil your domestic peace and happiness. Tell your neighbour or your mother that a visit right now is not convenient and suggest a time when you can visit her at her house instead; then you can decide when it's time to come home.

The growing family

● Sharing private time with your partner can be a particularly sensitive issue if the children of his or her previous marriage are living with you, as jealousy and resentment can easily result if you seem to be claiming your partner's attention at their expense. Children of a broken marriage need to remain close to both their parents, and any behaviour of yours that shuts them out will be felt as a serious threat. You and your partner need to be united in your firmness about private time and space, so that the children know where they stand, but they will only be happy with this as long as your attitude does not make them feel excluded. Spend time getting to know and like them, not just in your partner's company but when he or she is not there, and you will gradually gain their trust, respect and even affection.

If the children's lives are split between their divorced parents, include their time spent away from home and their relationship with your partner's ex-husband or wife in your conversation. It is unfair and harmful to expect a child to edit out such an important part of her life for your convenience. However much reports of the ex-spouse irk you, don't forget that the child loves this person, and is looking to you for affirmation.

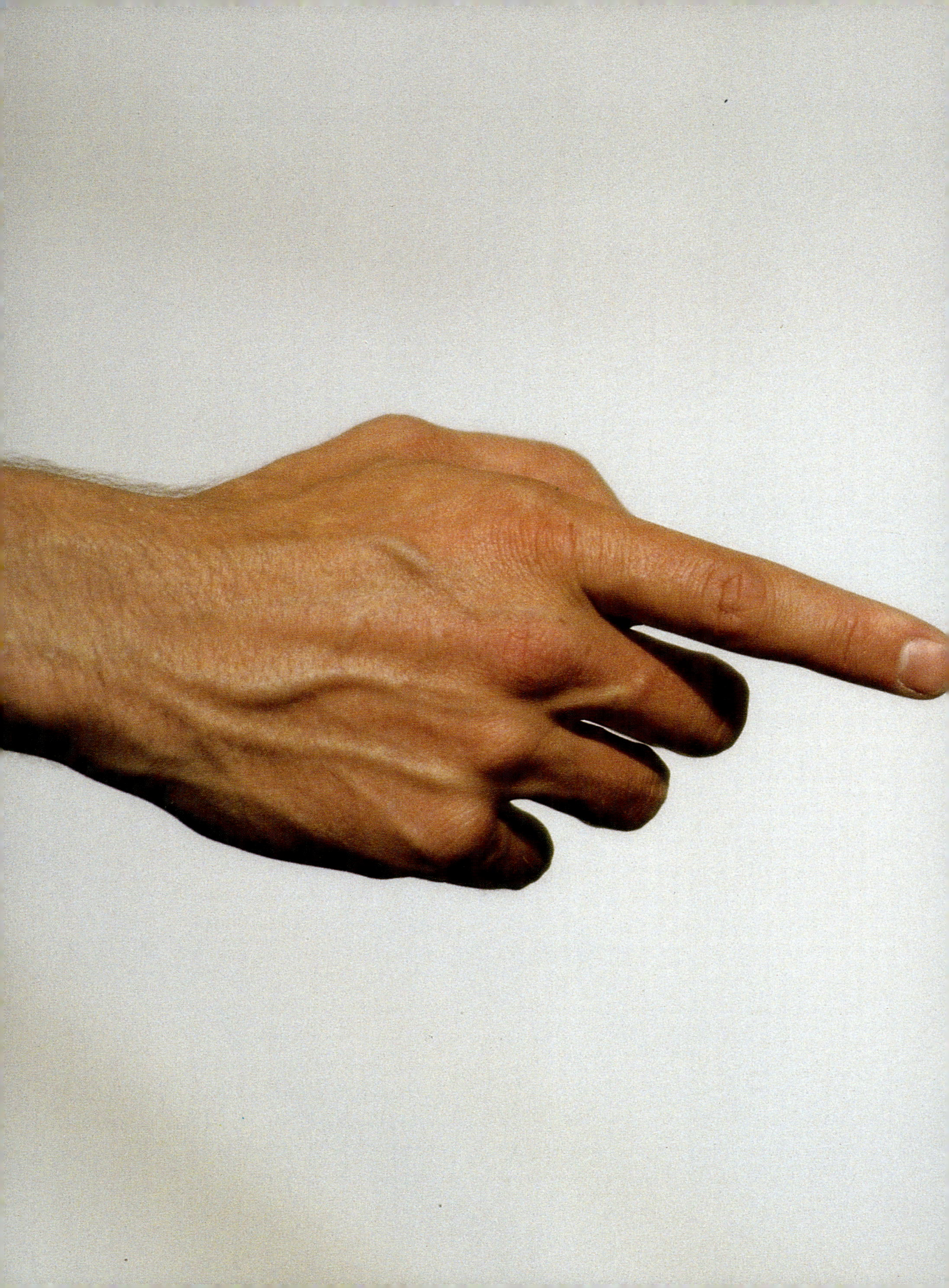

staying in touch

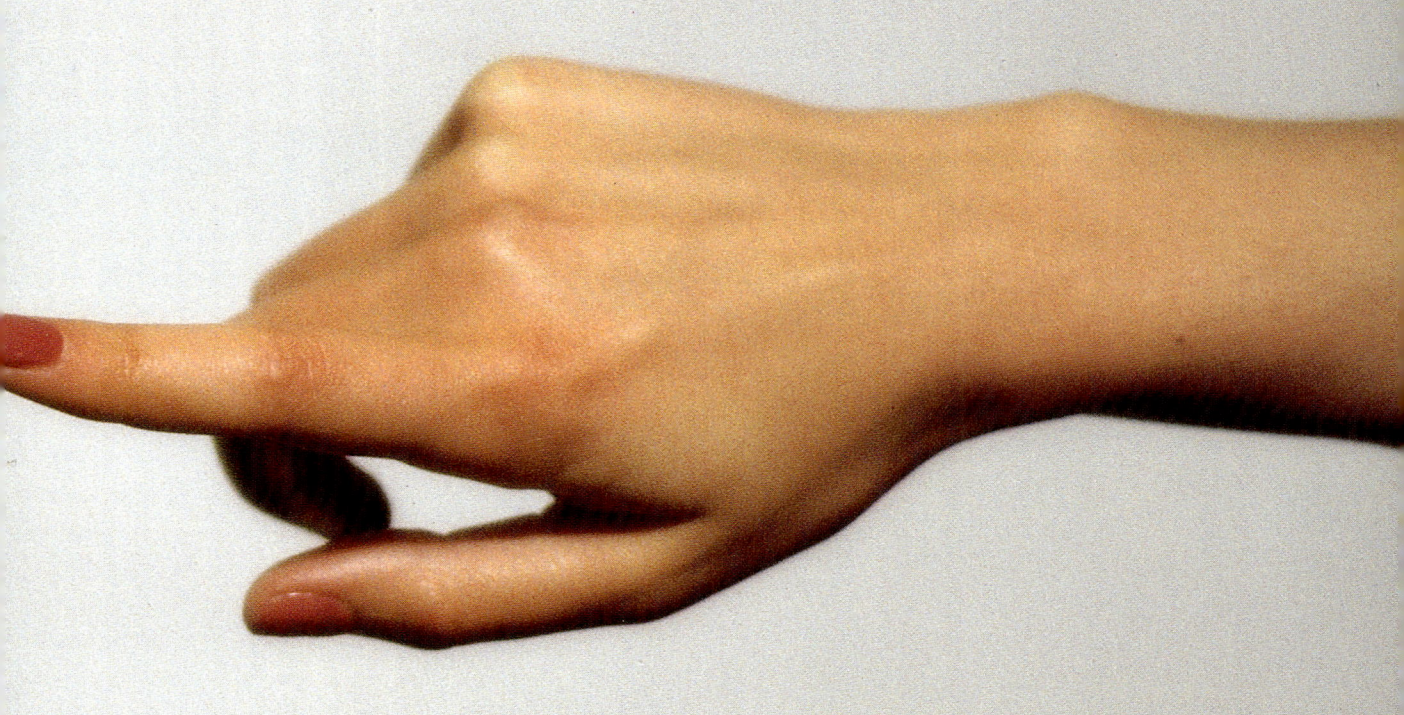

Keeping your relationship alive

New relationships are full of the excitement of exploration and discovery: being in love makes you vulnerable, you take emotional risks, you delight in new-found sharing, you are constantly developing and learning.

At some point along this path comes commitment, sometimes symbolized by marriage, at other times not. Gradually, living together, the process of 'learning each other' becomes complete.

It is easy to tell just by observing their behaviour in public what stage of their relationship a couple are in. The early stages are marked by physical closeness: standing, lying or sitting together, with or without touching. The pair are seen to occupy a common space, which others are not welcome to invade. Often, young lovers embrace or kiss in public, and new lovers of any age touch each other frequently and display other signs of attentiveness, looking at each other a lot and holding prolonged eye contact.

Before the couple have taken the decisive step of making love, there is often continuous animated conversation, as each gives the other a 'map' of past history, anecdotes and information about friends and relations, sharing life before they met. Once they have become lovers, the couple grow more secure in each other, and can relax in periods of blissful silence, merely basking in each other's company.

Couples who have been together a long time may not at first look like a couple. Because they have learned each other's reactions they no longer need to watch out for them: they know instinctively what their partners think and feel and can confirm their mutual understanding with the most fleeting glance. These small signs signify a submerged wealth of shared experience.

Other couples, unaware of the need to

Keeping your relationship alive

nurture their relationship to keep it alive, exhibit signs of having grown apart. In public they often appear bored or frustrated in each other's company; in private they listen with half an ear, grunt in reply, and retreat from communication by watching the television or going out to pursue a private interest. Yet they too were once in love. So what has happened to them? And what can be done to keep your relationship alive?

How healthy is your relationship?

Healthy relationships are based on mutual liking, caring and sexual attraction. If these three vital elements cease to be felt and expressed, the life blood of the relationship dries up and just the empty shell remains. The couple may go on saying 'I love you' out of habit, but it now means little more than 'I am used to you'.

Many couples slip from passion to tolerance over the years because they don't bother to affirm their feelings for each other. Marriage can make people lazy. The excitement of courtship over, they relax their attention on the relationship and concentrate on something else: work, leisure interests, raising a family. Promising to love each other for ever is not a guarantee that this will happen automatically. Ask yourself what you mean by love. Do you like your partner? Do you care for him? Does he turn you on?

The importance of liking

It's difficult to love someone you don't like. And it's difficult not to like some-

---

How alive is your relationship?

1. Do you have interesting conversations with your partner?
2. Do you talk about the state of your relationship?
3. If you have them, are the children your main topic of conversation?
4. Do you find your partner predictable to the point where it's not worth listening?
5. Do you often surprise your partner?
6. Do your favourite leisure activities involve your partner?
7. Is most of your free time spent performing domestic or DIY chores/working on the car/garden?
8. When you relax together, is it most often in front of the television?
9. Is your sex life with your partner exciting?
10. Does your partner make you laugh?

If you've answered honestly, you will want to do something about 'yes' answers to numbers 3, 4, 7 and 8.

---

one whose company you enjoy. Make sure you don't give up the things you enjoyed doing together at the beginning. Your shared interests will keep you close. The only shared interest some couples have is watching television. Unless used very discriminatingly, the television can dominate your home and numb your emotional life by making it unnecessary or impossible to talk to one another. Sitting in front of the television night after night is a way of giving up responsibility towards your partner.

Find something in which you can both participate: go to art classes, out to a restaurant or the pub, join a drama group or a political organization, learn a language, take up cycling or photography. Above all, talk to each other and make each other laugh. The evening meal forms the focal point of most couples' days: sharing the planning, cooking and eating of it offers a good opportunity to appreciate each other's talent, fortitude and sense of humour.

Accept that your feelings towards your partner are a living force that fluctuates according to your moods and actions, and that sometimes you may like him to a pitch of delight, and at other times you may like him less. Whenever you really like your partner, make sure you tell him so. It's refreshing and realistic to be told 'I do like you so much', or 'You are so funny'. Such positive and specific compliments often give a bigger boost to the ego than being told 'I love you'.

BEING AWARE: CARING

Really liking someone makes it easy to care for them. Care is the nourishment that close relationships need in order to thrive – it involves continuing to look after your partner's physical and emotional wellbeing. With thoughtfulness and imagination you can anticipate some of your partner's needs and desires; and your conversations should reveal other ways in which you can be supportive.

Encourage your partner to share problems with you, and in turn be open about the issues that are worrying you. You can't be expected to understand the minutiae of each other's situation at work, but professional and even technical problems all have a human angle that may be more obvious to the eye of the one who is not immersed in them. Just the act of explaining your problem to someone who listens with a sympathetic ear will lessen the burden.

Caring for each other is often a practical thing. Remembering that you're performing chores in order to create an environment in which you can be happy together can take the drudgery out of them; if it doesn't, question their necessity, or at least the thoroughness and regularity with which you perform them.

Creative caring involves generosity and spontaneity; it means pulling off the blinkers of routine and being aware of your partner's fluctuations of mood. It's being able to drop what you're doing to lend a helping hand, or give advice, or a shoulder to cry on, or just a smile of wry understanding – whatever is appropriate – in the knowledge that your partner will also always be available for you.

AFFIRMING ATTRACTION

The capacity for passion does not diminish with increasing age. If your relationship is no longer mutually sexually satisfying, it doesn't mean that either of you is no longer capable of enjoying exciting sex. A couple who no longer make

Staying in touch

love, or who have gradually formed a habit of having sex without total emotional involvement, have made a space in their lives in which interest in other people can take root. While your relationship may survive infidelity (see page 72), an affair will change it irrevocably, whether it is discovered or not.

Affairs start because of stagnation and boredom. Of course, no relationship can remain at the pitch of feverish excitement that marked its initial stages. But there is no doubt that however good sex is at the beginning, it can get better, deeper, stronger. A good sexual relationship takes a long time to develop. Its development is something to look forward to and to nurture. Both men and women need time in which to learn the responses of their partner's body; time in which to open up and come to trust each other, so that their own responses can happen naturally and spontaneously.

In a fully developed sexual relationship, techniques – different ways of touching, moving and embracing – that the partners have taught each other and learned together, marry perfectly with an understanding of each other's moods and needs. Sex then becomes a deep and powerful wordless communication of feeling. Sex should be infinite in its variety, just with the one partner. The more finely you are attuned to each other, the more subtle the nuances of feeling you will be able to arouse. The more gently experimental you are, the more powerful responses you will invite.

Couples who are fully sexually aware of each other don't need to be in bed together to feel it or express it. They convey sexual awareness in the way they look, speak, and in the way they touch. Other emotions may crowd to the fore, but sexuality informs the dynamics of the relationship. It is always there, so when you put your arms around each other, you can tell the second the hug melts into an erotic embrace. If it's appropriate, allow your feelings to become fully sexual; if not, anticipate fulfilling them at another time; that way, you can break off without feelings of rejection.

STAYING ATTRACTIVE

Your personality takes its expression in your appearance, and your appearance will have been one of the first things about you to attract your partner. Looking good boosts your confidence; it makes you feel good, and it makes your partner feel good to be with you. Taking care of your appearance should be a pleasure as well as a matter of self-respect. However, some people tend to let themselves go once they settle with a partner. Maybe they feel that their power to earn money or their hard work keeping house and raising a family will replace physical attractiveness as the tie that binds.

Whatever your age and looks, make the most of yourself. Start by paying attention to diet and fitness. If you are looking after children, don't eat their leftovers; if you are constantly expected to eat business lunches, eat sensibly. Discuss diet and fitness together and draw up a plan. Take up some form of exercise such as yoga, aerobics, or swimming that you can share.

STAYING INTERESTING

- *Say only what you mean; mean what you say.*
- *Only say 'I love you' when the feeling is current: accept the fact that feelings ebb and flow.*
- *Don't complain: this will grate. Air problems and discuss solutions.*
- *Don't assume you've heard it all before – listen to what your partner is telling you.*
- *Don't bore your partner by talking at length about hobbies that don't interest her.*
- *Share new plans with your partner.*
- *Make plans together.*
- *Make time to talk and enjoy one another's company undisturbed.*
- *Don't relegate sex to bedtime, or sexuality to the bedroom.*
- *Break your routines, and introduce an element of surprise into your relationship.*
- *Don't stop celebrating.*
- *Stay attractive.*

Understanding stress

We all thrive under a certain amount of stress: it gives a biting edge to life and enables us to enjoy our own power to stay on top, but too much stress and life gets out of control.

Many of us work better to a deadline, and most enjoy a thrill of adrenalin on meeting a challenge, but an unremitting build-up of stress over a long period of time is destructive, and can cause serious and even fatal illness.

WHAT CAUSES STRESS AND HOW TO RECOGNIZE IT

We usually think of stress as being caused by the continual harrassment or worry of problems at work or at home, and by environmental factors such as noise pollution, bad air, overcrowding and traffic. But it can also be caused by events that 'ought' to bring only happiness. The build-up of expectation and nervous anxiety that attend the preparations for a wedding, the birth of a baby, or even a holiday or family Christmas can put a lot of pressure on all concerned. Tempers fray, and the feeling of frustration is exacerbated by the knowledge that planning a celebration should be fun. Partners can take a lot of the strain off each other by working together to organize things, and by keeping a sense of humour. That's much easier to do if there are two of you involved.

Stress is insidious: it can easily build up without your being aware of it. After all, you are probably too distracted to notice your own symptoms. Although you may realize your energy reserves are low, it may take your partner to point out other symptoms.

DO DRUG TREATMENTS WORK?

Drug companies have cashed in on the fact that stress causes more diseases in our society than viruses or bacteria. In the 1960s they developed a group of drugs called benzodiazepines, which were hailed by doctors as an instant cure for stress and prescribed to millions of patients. Taking tranquillizers became

Understanding stress

commonplace: lifelong addictive habits were formed. Now each year doctors in the UK write around 30 million prescriptions for drugs such as Valium, Librium, Ativan and Mogadon, and around three million Britons, i.e. 6 per cent of the population, rely on them every day.

However, benzodiazepines are addictive. And ironically, they produce side-effects such as anxiety, depression and sleeplessness: the very conditions they are intended to cure. Coming off tranquillizers is as difficult as coming off any other addictive drug. The patient is likely to suffer unpleasant withdrawal symptoms, such as giddiness, panic attacks, shaking and insomnia. And, of course, once you have weaned yourself off the drugs, you still have to tackle the underlying cause of stress, because drugs work by suppressing the symptoms, not by effecting a cure. Stress is caused by an emotional reaction to lifestyle, and it's not a problem that can be driven off by pumping chemicals into the bloodstream.

SYMPTOMS OF STRESS

WHAT YOU FEEL
- *headache*
- *chest pain*
- *exhaustion*
- *insomnia*
- *palpitations*
- *skin rash*
- *lethargy*
- *lack of enthusiasm*
- *indigestion*
- *diarrhoea*

WHAT YOUR PARTNER OBSERVES
- *that you can't relax*
- *you can't concentrate*
- *you are forgetful*
- *often near to tears*
- *intolerant and irritable*
- *loss of appetite*
- *loss of libido*

So what can be done to relieve stress?

The first and most obvious solution is to try to remove or resolve whatever is causing the stress. Perhaps you can sort out a long-running dispute, cut down on the number of hours you work, delegate responsibility? Discussing your problems with your partner will do you both good; kept to yourself, they block communication and your partner will feel cut off and powerless to help.

If you can't get rid of the problem, can you at least distance yourself from it emotionally? Some people worry needlessly about affairs that are outside their control, or which should not affect them so acutely. Again, talk to your partner to get a fresh angle on this. Or can you distance yourself physically from the problem at intervals, and for long enough to make a complete recovery from stress? If work gets you down, can you spend time at the weekends enjoying an utterly different environment with your partner? Instead of filling your spare time with a round of chores around the house and garden, you should make an effort to get away.

Sharing an absorbing weekend

interest will bring you closer and help you forget the cares of the week so that you can return to work refreshed and ready for a new challenge. Consider planning long walks or cycle rides, exploring new areas of the surrounding countryside. Water is a most relaxing element: some therapists recommend immersion in a darkened saline tank for the ultimate relaxing experience, but you may think sailing, canoeing or swimming more enjoyable.

Completely private time to oneself is a very underrated tonic for stress. If you are in a relationship, particularly if you have a family, making time for yourself in which to do absolutely nothing except sit in a chair or lie in the bath and stare, and let your mind float free of clutter into pure daydream, may seem selfish, if not impossible. However, as a restorative, it's as useful as meditation, and it's something you can give to each other.

All you need is a couple of hours alone and absolute quiet. Unplug the phone. Disconnect the doorbell. Don't feel guilty that you're wasting time: just let your mind go blank. After the rubbish has stopped churning round you will find a new kind of peace. Images and fragments of thought surface in a fluid unstructured activity and that's very different to conscious thought. In this state you are likely to be surprised by some of your most creative ideas: solutions to problems that may have been worrying you for weeks suddenly and unexpectedly spring fully formed to the surface of your mind.

Tension creates a bad, cramped posture, and this can be corrected by learning how to sit, stand and move in a relaxed way. Then you can learn deep breathing and muscle relaxation: techniques that you can use to help you centre yourself in moments of crisis.

TENSION AND BODY LANGUAGE

We can all read signs of tension in other people: they stand hunched up, sit with their legs twisted round and round, fiddle, chew their fingers, etc. The trouble is, we can't usually recognize these things in ourselves – unless someone else is brave enough to point them out. Body language reflects the way we feel about ourselves and the world around us. Anxiety is reflected in awkwardness and contorted limbs, and in behaviour that's markedly aggressive or defensive. Someone who feels at ease with themselves will present a figure that's neither bolt upright nor slouching; conversely, someone who adopts a relaxed bearing will automatically feel more at ease.

- *To check your own bearing, stand in front of a mirror with your feet comfortably apart and your weight evenly distributed between them. Let your arms hang naturally at your sides. Now straighten your spine, right from your coccyx to the base of your neck. You will probably be able to feel the difference, which means that your bearing could be more relaxed and comfortable than it is. Repeat the exercise, but sitting down, with your hands in your lap and your feet on the floor. Correct your way of standing and sitting every time you remember it, until you have trained yourself to do it automatically.*

- *Pay special attention to your head and neck. Your head is very heavy (5-6 kg/12-14 lb), and if you don't hold it dead-centre it can cause muscle strain and even migraine. Get your partner to tell you if you have a habit of holding your head on one side.*

- *People who risk muscle strain in their jobs, such as hairdressers and dentists, need to do stretching exercises to compensate for cramped posture at work. You should also do compensating exercises if you overuse one side of your body, by lifting heavy weights or playing sport.*

Understanding stress

DEEP BREATHING AND MUSCLE RELAXATION

There is a direct connection between deep breathing and muscle relaxation. When you are tense, your muscles are clenched and your breathing is fast and shallow. This is what happens when you are geared up for 'fight or flight', and your heart races and adrenalin pumps through your body. The body behaves quite differently when it is relaxed. Observing your partner asleep, you will notice that his breathing is deep, his limbs are heavy, and all the tension has disappeared from his face. Relaxation, especially over a holiday, actually makes everyone look younger.

Whenever you feel tense or nervous, breathe in and out, slowly and deeply, two or three times, concentrating on filling your lungs completely with air and letting it out gradually again. This simple calming exercise is practised regularly by public speakers and performers and can be put to good use without anyone noticing what you are doing.

relaxation techniques

How do you relax with your partner? Most people spend a fair amount of their time together in front of the television. But watching television can be just a way of blocking out the tensions of the day, or the tensions between the two of you.

Television is commonly used as a suppressant. Switch it on, let it absorb your attention and numb your awareness of your surroundings. Switch it off, and those tensions will crowd back in on you again. You may feel tired after an evening of television, you may stretch and yawn because you've been sitting in one position for too long, you may be exhausted and want to go to bed. But true relaxation is not feeling 'knackered'; it's a delicate balance that involves feeling free of tension and energized at the same time. It's a state of heightened bodily awareness and wellbeing, of feeling revitalized and refreshed. It's the best state to be in if you want to make love, or if you want to drift off into a blissful sleep.

When you're on holiday, it's easy to relax. You have time to dawdle and enjoy yourselves, time to linger over food and drink, time to read, swim or just bask. And you will notice how being relaxed together enables you to communicate better, and to have better sex. But holidays are few and far between, and the stresses of everyday life are such that an hour spent relaxing here and there brings little relief.

Paradoxically, you need to make a bigger effort to relax. Ideally, you should set aside some time each day to practise a method of deep relaxation that will rid you of the pressures and trivialities that block communication and cause sleepless nights. The methods of relaxation described on the next pages can all be practised together. The yoga sequence (page 142) is useful at either end of the day, but particularly before bed – as long as you haven't just eaten an enormous meal. Massage is for special occasions as well as to soothe tension from knotted muscles. Try the aromatherapy oils (page 140) to stimulate, and heal as well as to help you relax.

Relaxation techniques

Massage:
A WAY OF GETTING IN TOUCH

People who lead busy and stressful lives tend to withdraw and focus their energy inwards on their own preoccupations, rather than out towards their partner. They forget to touch each other except during sex. Yet touching and caressing are important ways of showing recognition and acceptance and of communicating how much you care. For a couple who have literally 'lost touch', massage offers a way of making contact and of getting to know each other's bodies again.

Rhythmically stroking another person to bring relaxation and comfort is the oldest and simplest form of therapy in the world. Massage relieves nervous tension and relaxes knotted muscles, improving circulation and body tone and inducing a feeling of wellbeing and wholeness. In an intimate relationship, massage can flood into tender and erotic feelings, or send your partner drifting into a peaceful and rejuvenating sleep. You can use it to heal and soothe if you are tense and tired or suffering from aching limbs, or to clear and concentrate the mind and relax the body if you are wide awake but as yet too tense and distracted to make love. Massage can be as beneficial for the giver as for the receiver if both parties concentrate themselves solely on the point of contact.

BEFORE YOU BEGIN

The requirements for massage are simple. You will need a warm quiet room free of draughts and intrusions such as the radio and telephone. The atmosphere should be relaxing, the light dim: perhaps candlelight or firelight.

You both need to be comfortable. The receiver should lie on a firm surface, such as the floor or your bed or a large sturdy table, covered with rugs or blankets, and then a towel. Use another towel to cover the parts of the body you aren't working on, if you wish. To give a massage, you should stand, sit or kneel in a balanced position, as any awkwardness or tension will transmit directly to your partner, as well as bothering you. A massage oil or cream will enable your hands to glide smoothly over your partner's body. The most luxurious oils are those used for aromatherapy (see page 138), but you could also use almond oil or baby oil. Keep the oil close to you, but put it where you won't knock it over. Warm it before use by rubbing it between your palms: never drip it directly on to your partner's body. Take off all your jewellery and check that your nails are short and not sharp.

The most essential preparation for giving a massage is to centre yourself. Remember that the laying on of hands is an ancient form of healing. Everyone has the power to give, and the more you are aware of it, the better you will be able to transmit it. The Japanese have a word, *hara*, which means lower abdomen. They believe that this is the centre of the body, from which power flows. Focus yourself on this centre and allow the power to spread through your body and arms to your fingertips. Relax your hands and wrists by shaking them. While you are massaging your partner, keep your back straight and move from your pelvis. Always keep yourself aware of the power in your hands.

Massage strokes

Begin with a featherlight touch, but avoid tickling, and gradually increase in concentration and pressure until you reach below the soft flesh and the superficial muscles to massage the joints. Once you have felt the knots of tension dissolving under your touch, you can gradually relax the pressure and end as lightly as you began.

If you are going to move on to an erotic massage, don't rush. Make sure your partner is thoroughly relaxed before you make any moves that might arouse him or her. You could begin with a complete back massage with deep pressure, then work lightly and gently down the chest to the belly and upper thighs, circling tantalizingly in towards the genitals. Don't allow your partner to join in, but continue with rhythmic stimulation, following the movements you know he or she enjoys during masturbation, until orgasm is reached.

● *LIGHT STROKES are used to begin and end a massage and to move from one part of the body to another. They should be broad, fluent and soothing, pouring generously like warm water over the flesh. Mould your palms and fingers into the contours of your partner's body and break contact only when necessary, and then as gently as possible.*

● *DEEPER STROKES follow once your partner is used to your touch. Pull and knead the flesh rhythmically, with one hand echoing the movement of the other. Stretch the flesh under your hands, then let it relax. Don't grab, but keep your hands on the body, rocking back on the heel of your hand between movements.*

● *THE MOST PENETRATING STROKES follow once your partner is completely relaxed. Work concentratedly with the ball of your thumb, your fingertips and the heel of your hand. Push rhythmically, describing tiny circles and feeling for knotted muscles. Use your full body weight and be as firm as you can without hurting your partner.*

Step-by-Step Massage

*Use the steps below as a guide on which you can improvise.
Repeat each step as many times as you like, and on the other side of the body.*

The Back

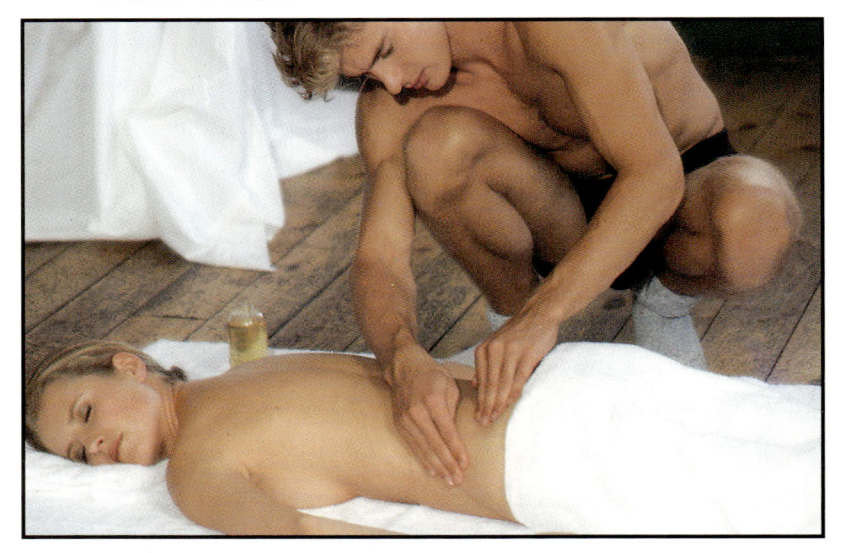

ONE. Start on the side of the body opposite you. Work from the small of the back, massaging down the sides and up to the shoulder blades.

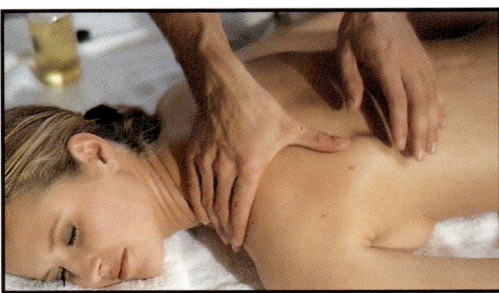

TWO. Work around the shoulder blade with the whole hand, pushing away from the spine with firm strokes.

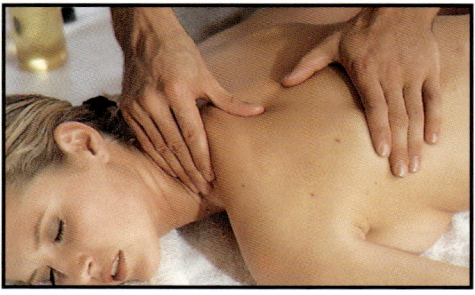

THREE. Pull the muscle towards you with your fingertips and circle under the shoulder blade with the flat of your hand.

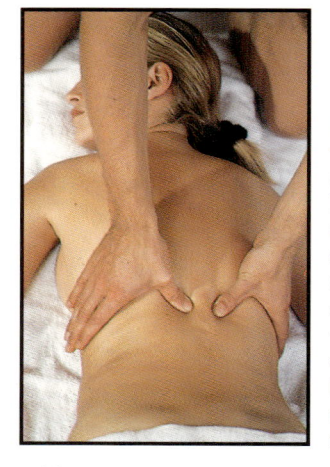

FOUR. Position yourself at the top of your partner's head and with thumbs on either side of the spine (not on the spine, on the muscle), work down towards the buttocks with small circular movements.

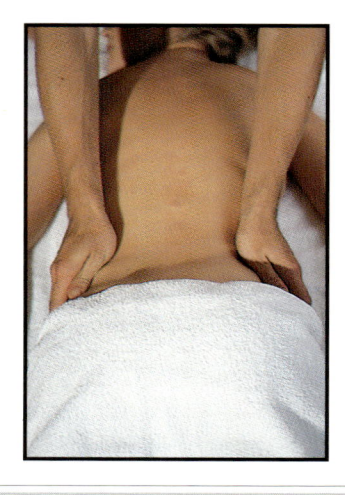

FIVE. Smooth down the back with the flat of the hand, being careful to avoid the spine.

Step-by-step massage

BACKS OF LEGS AND ANKLES

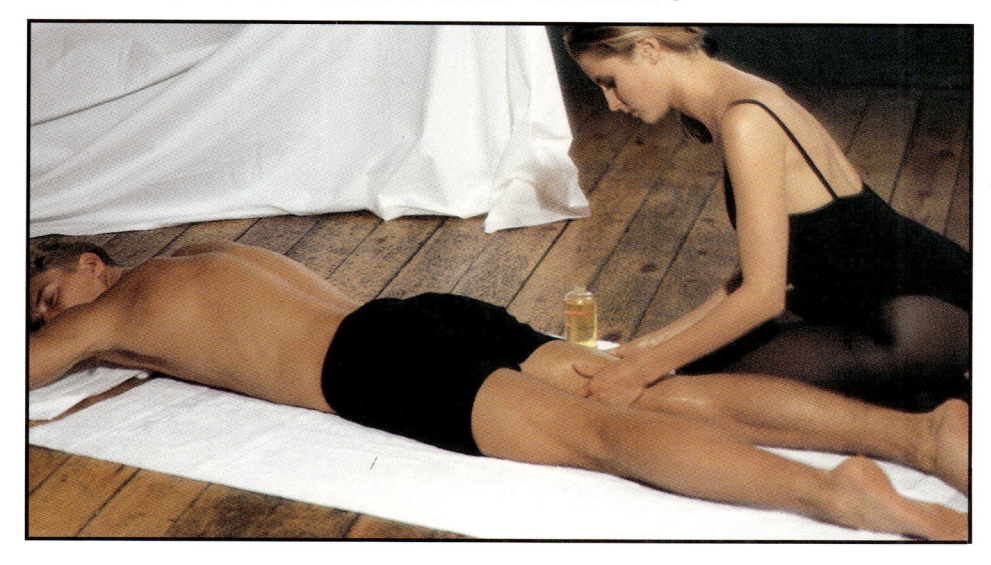

ONE. Place both hands on your partner's upper thigh. Use your thumbs to massage down the leg in small outward circles from the thigh down to the ankle, working on all the muscles as you go.

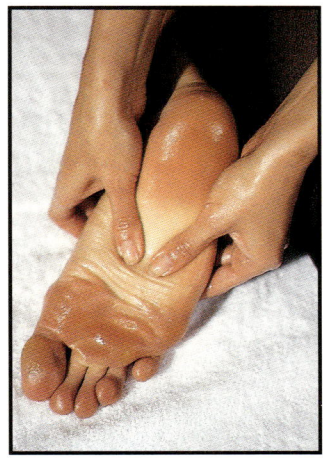

TWO. Continue on the foot, describing small outward spiralling circles. Press firmly enough not to tickle.

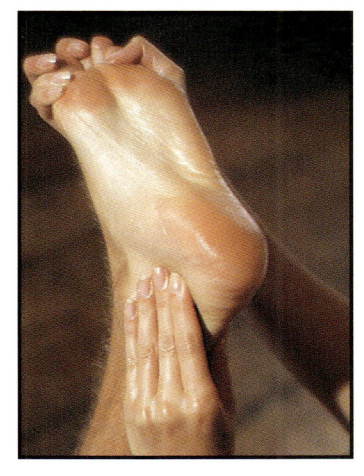

THREE. Bend the leg at the knee joint and stretch the foot carefully upwards. Rotate the ankle slowly and gently, first in one direction, then the other.

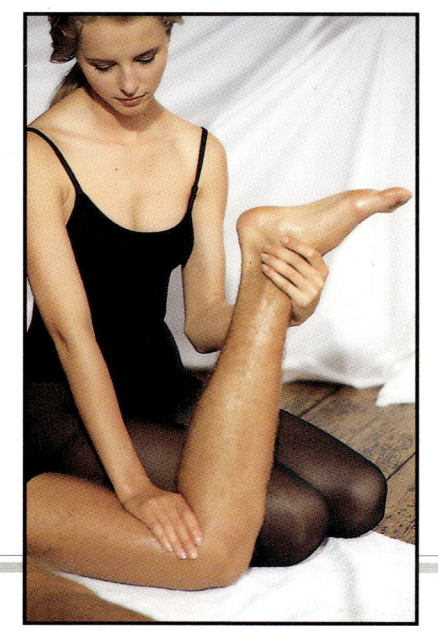

FOUR. Gently lift the leg and move it slowly from side to side. Do not force it. Stop if your partner feels uncomfortable.

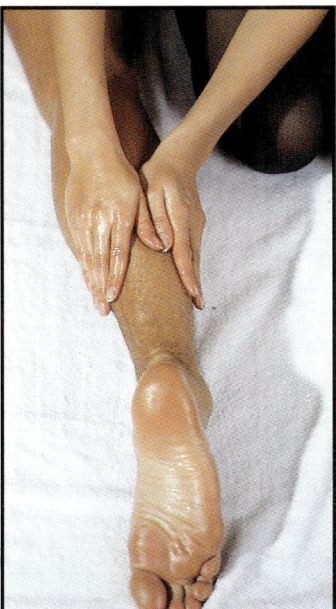

FIVE Lower the leg and finish with long firm strokes from thigh to ankle.

133

Arms and hands

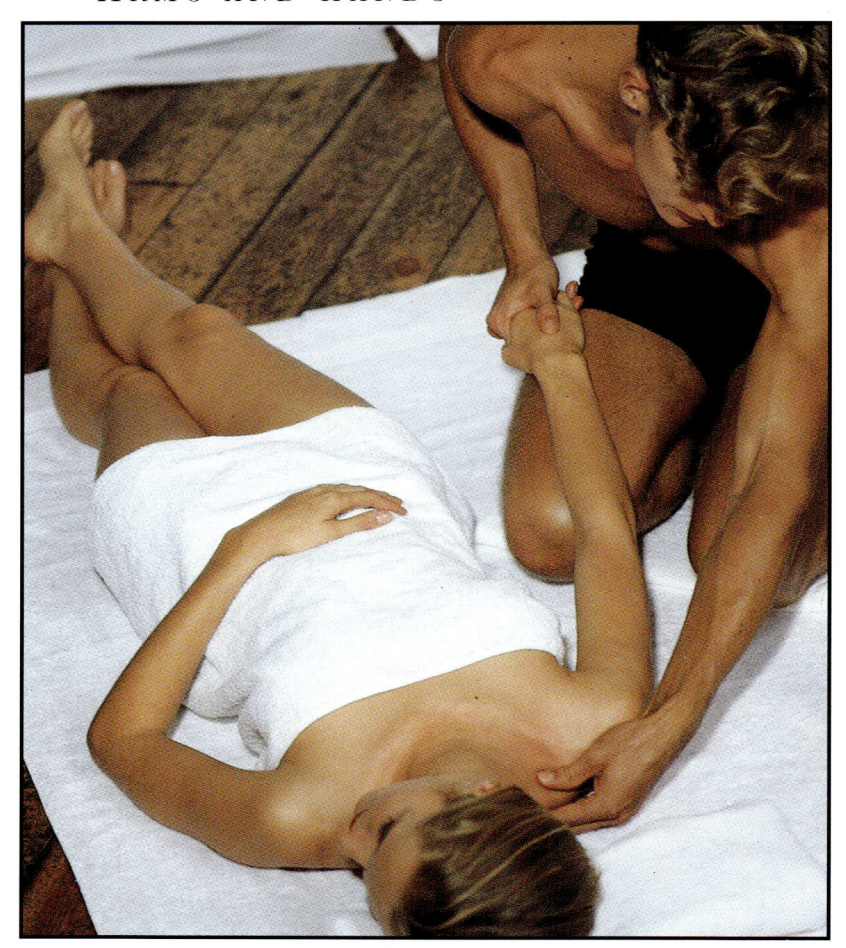

ONE. Your partner now lies on his back. Hold the hand nearest you and massage the muscle between the shoulder and the neck with your thumb.

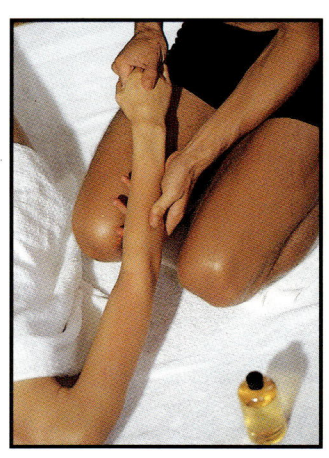

TWO. Work with your thumb all the way down the front of the arm to the hand. Repeat down the back of the arm.

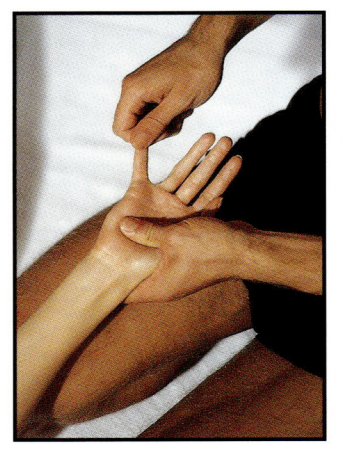

THREE. Massage the hand and fingers with tiny circular thumb movements. Gently stretch and rotate the fingers, first in one direction, then in the other.

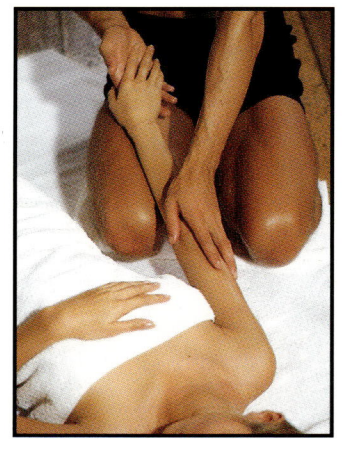

FOUR. Finish with long firm strokes from the shoulder to the fingers.

Step-by-step massage

CHEST AND ABDOMEN

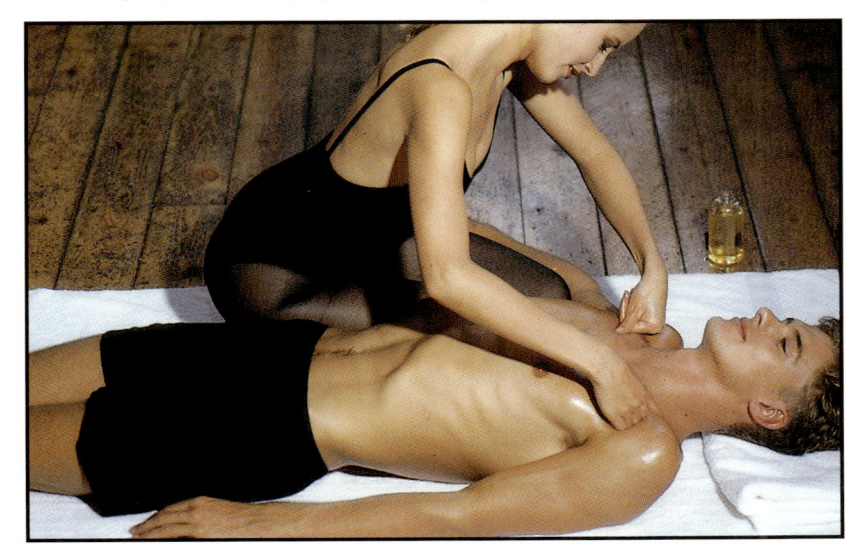

ONE. Massage the chest muscles below the collar bone with your thumb.

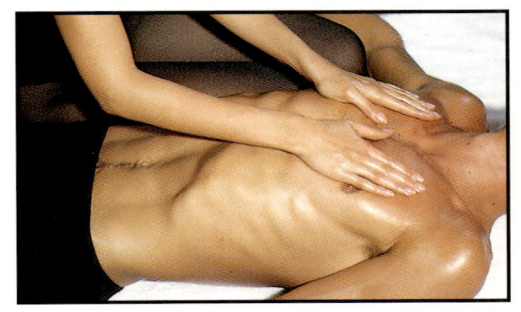

TWO. Circulate with the flat of your hand round the breast and rib area.

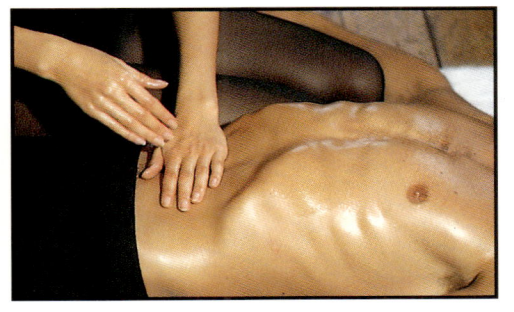

THREE. Again with the flat of the hand, pull diagonally across the abdomen.

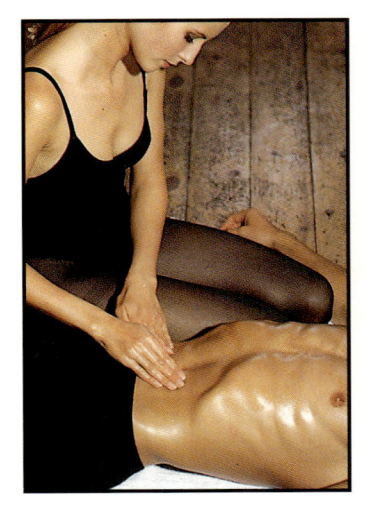

FOUR. Make gentle circular strokes on your partner's abdomen with your fingertips. Work outwards and clockwise.

FIVE. To finish, hold your partner's sides firmly and gently while he breathes deeply in and out.

Front of legs and feet

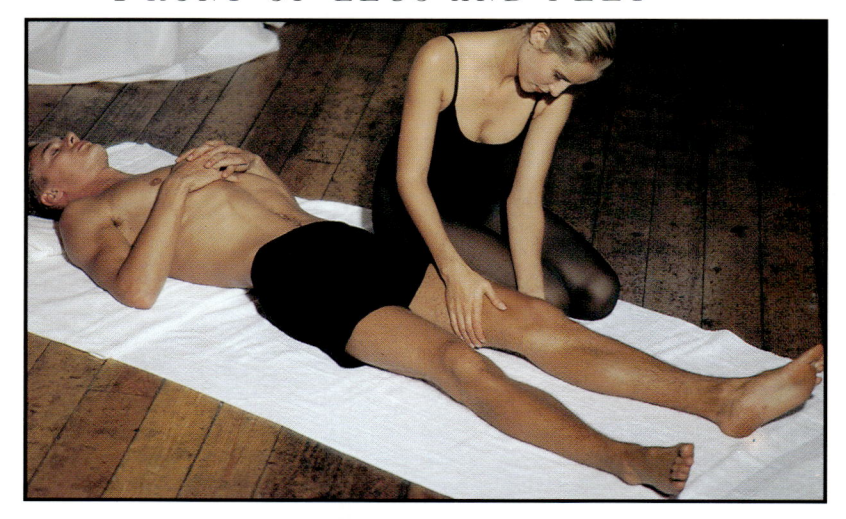

One. Support the back of your partner's knee with one hand. Follow the contour of the thigh muscle with the thumb of your other hand, working in a diagonal from the inside of the knee to the hip.

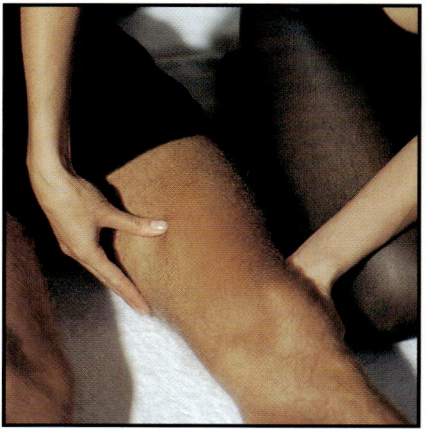

Two. With your thumb, work on the muscle of the outer thigh in small circular movements. Repeat on the inner thigh.

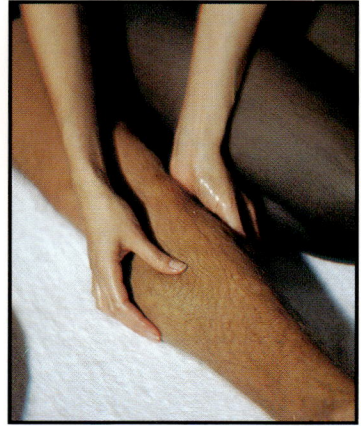

Three. Using both hands, massage down the calf muscle with circular thumb movements and all the way down to the foot on both sides of the leg.

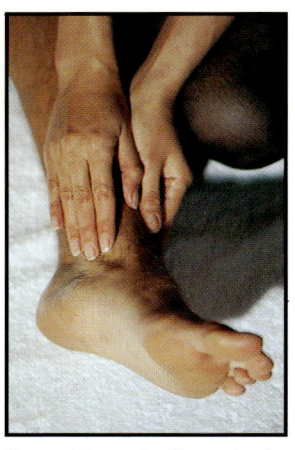

Four. Move the fingertips in small circles round the ankle bone.

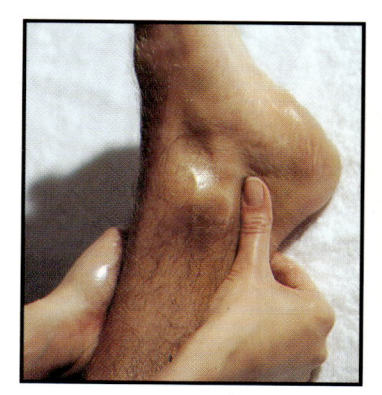

Five. Massage the inner heel with rotating thumb movements on each side of the foot.

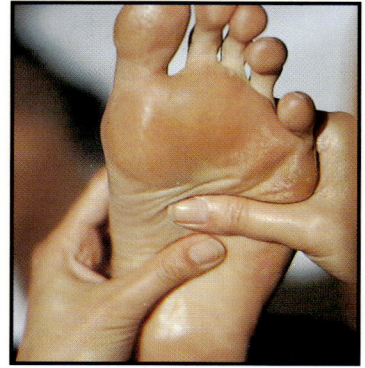

Six. Massage the sole of the foot with your thumb, pressing firmly. Work upwards to the toes.

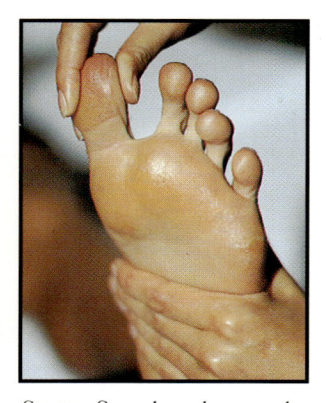

Seven. Stretch each toe and rotate it gently, first in one direction, then the other.

Step-by-step massage

NECK, HEAD AND FACE

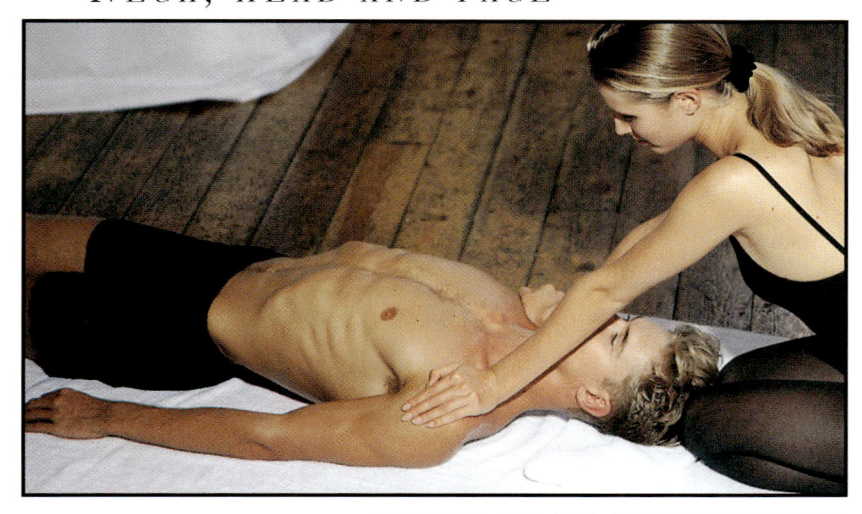

ONE Position yourself at the top of your partner's head and push down firmly but gently on the shoulders with the heels of your hands.

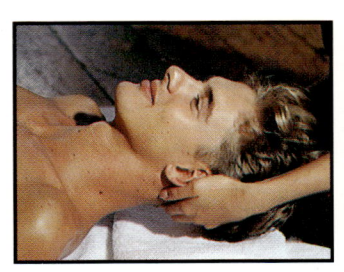

TWO. Lift your partner's head and gently stretch his neck. Position his head with chin up so you can get your hands behind his neck. Massage the back of his neck with your fingertips.

THREE. Work over the scalp with the fingertips of both hands, as if you were washing his hair.

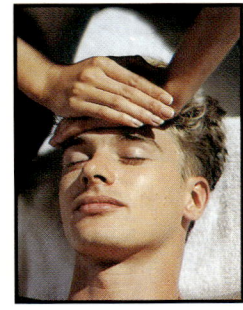

FOUR. Rest your hands on your partner's forehead while he breathes deeply, then smooth your thumbs to the centre of the brow and away again several times, moving with his breathing.

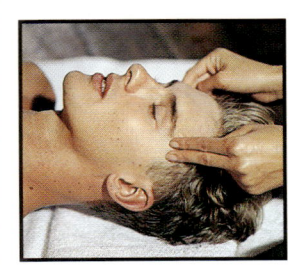

FIVE. Circulate your thumbs on the temples in small gentle movements.

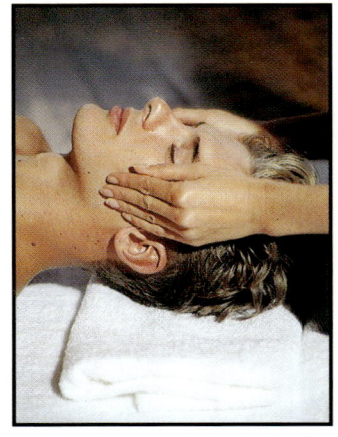

SIX. Gently smooth the flesh of the face upwards and outwards from cheek to chin with your fingertips.

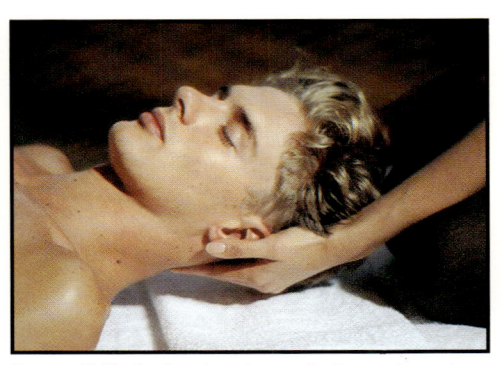

SEVEN. Lift the head and stretch the neck again, turning the head gently from side to side.

EIGHT. Finish by pulling your fingers gently upwards through his hair.

Staying in touch

AROMATHERAPY AND OTHER TREATS OF NATURE

Massage leads quite naturally into pampering your partner, male or female, in other imaginative ways. Don't be afraid to make and accept loving gestures that may at first seem absurdly over-indulgent. When your partner is slumped in a chair after a long walk or a tiring trek round the shops, surprise him by bringing a bowl of warm water, soap and a towel and gently washing his aching feet: there could be no more welcome or moving testimony of your feelings. Or soap his body for him when he's in the bath or shower, or give him a blanket bath with hot flannels after making love, or wash his hair with a long and luxurious massage of the scalp, and then brush and blow it dry.

Men also love to luxuriate in intimate attention that is both gentle and sensual: entice him to some extravagant salon treatment at home. Make him a face pack (avocado mashed with a little olive oil: you can lick it off afterwards), and put cucumber slices on his eyes, then rub aromatherapy oils into his sports injuries, or into his neck knotted with tension from work. Introduce him to the pleasure of silk. Let your imagination devise new and highly personal ways of cherishing each other, of inducing sheer comfort and erotic bliss.

ESSENTIAL OILS

Aromatherapy is the art of using the essential oils of plants as a complete treatment for mental and physical health and beauty. The practice is thousands of years old and was probably first employed systematically in China. The ancient Indian medical discipline, the Ayurveda, which is still very much alive today, uses plant essences to combat infection, soothe inflammation and relieve tension and depression.

As with all branches of holistic medicine, aromatherapy treatments are specifically designed for each individual patient; nevertheless it is commonly agreed that certain oils lift the spirits, whereas others calm them, and that some are particularly good for the skin, whereas others relieve aches and pains or heal wounds (see page 140). These oils can safely be used at home and their soothing and stimulating properties bring an extra dimension of pleasure to pampering your partner.

The oils can be administered in several ways, and the treatment is luxurious. First, the oils should be diluted in a neutral carrier oil. To apply neat essential oil to the skin could cause a burn. You can buy oils ready diluted, but if you have the concentrated essence, it needs to be mixed in the proportion of 1:50 with a carrier such as almond, apricot, hazelnut, groundnut or safflower oil. Always store essential oils in tightly capped or stoppered dark glass bottles in a cool place or in the fridge. Essential oils are highly volatile, unlike fatty culinary oils, and will evaporate quickly if exposed to heat, light or air.

The diluted oils can be applied to the face and body and rubbed or massaged into the skin. The base of the spine and the back of the neck are particularly good application points for the relief of tension. You can also inhale directly from the bottle or add one or two drips to a bowl of just-boiled water, bend your head over it and drape a towel over your head and the bowl to keep in the steam. This is particularly effective when using peppermint or eucalyptus oil to relieve breathing problems. Another way to enjoy the oils is to add about ten drops to a bath. Make sure the water is at the temperature that suits you and your partner best and share a long relaxing soak, inhaling the perfume at the same time.

It is still not known how essential oils work. The volatile molecules they are composed of dissolve in oil or water. When released into the air they are inhaled in minute water droplets. At the top of the nose they are intercepted by the olfactory nerve cells – of which humans have around ten million – and from there their messages are transmitted to the brain. When rubbed into the skin, the aromatic molecules are absorbed into the body through its natural oil or sebum. Oils that both stimulate and relax are the best to use before making love.

A GUIDE TO 20 ESSENTIAL OILS

Oil of Basil
Good against insect stings and for headaches, anxiety, depression and fatigue.

Oil of Camomile
Relaxing, calming, sedative and anti-inflammatory; good for stress, insomnia, sunburn and rashes. Lifts melancholy.

Oil of Cinnamon Leaf
Antiseptic and a stimulant; good for colds, tiredness and loss of libido.

Oil of Clary Sage
Don't confuse this with oil of sage, which is poisonous and particularly harmful during pregnancy. Oil of clary sage is a good tonic for depression and fatigue.

Oil of Eucalyptus
A powerful antiseptic, it acts against airborne germs, stimulates the nervous system and clears the head. Good for colds, bronchial disorders, aches and pains.

Oil of Frankincense
Relaxing, rejuvenating, uplifting.

Oil of Geranium
Tonic, sedative and antiseptic, oil of geranium balances any complexion and is good for relieving anxiety.

Oil of Jasmine
Rich, exotic and sensual, jasmine is used in classic perfumes. Lifts the mood.

Oil of Juniper
Antiseptic, stimulating and relaxing; good for stress, fatigue and lack of energy. It has diuretic properties and is also used on greasy skin and hair. Avoid oil of juniper during pregnancy.

Oil of Lavender
One of the most useful essential oils, it is both stimulant and sedative. A powerful antiseptic and healant, good for burns, aches and pains, infections.

Oil of Lemon
Refreshing, stimulating, vitamin-rich, a powerful antiseptic and astringent.

Oil of Neroli
Relaxing and calming, this is good for nervous tension, anxiety and insomnia. Recommended for dry skin.

Oil of Patchouli
The base of many heavy perfumes, patchouli stimulates in small amounts and acts as a sedative when used more liberally.

Oil of Peppermint
Envigorates, refreshes, numbs pain and clears the head. Good for fatigue, headaches, PMT. Lifts depression. Powerful, so use sparingly.

Oil of Rose
Use against stress, tension and headaches. Lifts the spirits. Excellent for the older skin.

Oil of Rosemary
Stimulates the mind and body, envigorates and refreshes. Good for fatigue, depression, and all aches and pains.

Oil of Sandalwood
Acts as a sedative and as a stimulant and is the base of many woody perfumes. Strengthens the immune system. Good for insomnia.

Oil of Tea-Tree
An extremely powerful antiseptic, and good for cuts, burns, acne and any other skin infections. Use in a douche to treat thrush.

Oil of Thyme
A powerful antiseptic, used in gargles. Good for skin inflammations, and also fatigue, anxiety and headaches.

Oil of Ylang-Ylang
Acts best on the emotions, both stimulating and relaxing. Calms nervous tension and lifts negative moods.

OINTMENTS AND FRAGRANT WATERS

You can also make ointments and fragrant waters with essential oils. For an ointment, melt over heat one part of beeswax with five parts of carrier oil. Stir well to combine, then allow to cool. Stir in ten drops of plant essence and store in a tightly sealed jar in a cool dark place. Do not add the oil while the mixture is hot or it will evaporate. For a room or body spray, add about five drops of oil to one pint/600ml water. To scent a room you can also add a few drops of oil to a bowl of water near a radiator.

YOGA

Yoga stretches and tones the body, improving the functioning of muscles and joints. The spine becomes more flexible and the exercises also work on the internal organs, the glands and the nerves. Yoga is the world's most ancient system of personal development. It means 'joining': the joining of the body and the self to an unchanging reality that lies beyond. It is a process that enables the shedding of personal preoccupations and the clutter of everyday life.

It's difficult to get in touch emotionally with your partner when one or the other of you is distracted and tense. You both need to be centred – in touch with yourselves – before you can connect with each other. Yoga can help, because it enables you to relax. It's possible to be tense all the time without knowing it: even to lie rigidly in bed, grimly awaiting sleep, without realizing that mind and body are merely galvanized for the sound of the alarm clock and the next headlong rush into action. Try consciously tensing and relaxing your muscles to see just how keyed up you are.

Physical relaxation brings a feeling of wellbeing, as well as freedom from aches and pains, but yoga gives more than this, and as you continue to practise it it brings a sense of harmony and a peace of mind that are the prerequisites of true self-knowledge. Yoga provides a touchstone of security and stillness that will always enable you to get your bearings in the confusion of everyday life.

The exercise of yoga consists of getting into and out of a series of postures, or asanas. The movements are slow and graceful, never jerky. They extend your reach gradually and should never be forced. After a yoga session you should feel both thoroughly relaxed and full of energy, not exhausted and strained. Breathing is especially important to help you move correctly.

In performing the following sequence of 12 asanas, don't worry if you can't get into some of the positions at first. You will be able to achieve them in time as you become more supple. Imagine yourself forming the shapes in the illustrations, even if you can't achieve them.

The series of 12 asanas on pages 142 and 143 is traditionally performed at dawn, as a greeting to the sun. However, it's also an ideal exercise sequence that you and your partner can perform together to rid yourselves of the tensions of the day before you go to bed.

the sun salutation

Each bend or stretch in this series of exercises balances the one before, improving the flexibility of your spine and the suppleness of the muscles.

ONE. Stand with your back straight and your feet together. Press your palms together in the prayer position. Feel balanced. Exhale.

TWO. Inhale and stretch up your arms, arching your back from the waist and pressing your hips forward. Keep your legs straight and let your neck relax.

THREE. Exhale and bring your body forward and down so that your hands touch the floor. In time you should be able to press your palms alongside your feet.

FOUR. Inhale and push one leg out behind you, touching the floor with the balls of your toes and your knee. Stretch your leg and arch your back. Lift your chin to form a continuous curve.

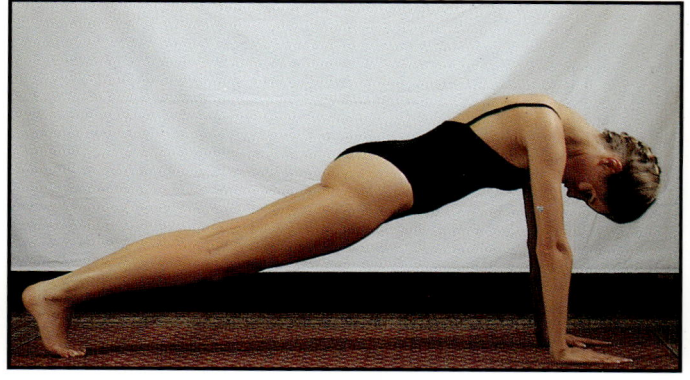

FIVE. Holding your breath, stretch the second leg back to join the first. Raise yourself up on hands and feet. Keep your body in a straight line, looking down between your hands.

SIX. Exhale, lowering yourself to the ground – first the knees, then the chest, then the forehead. Keep your toes curled and your hips raised.

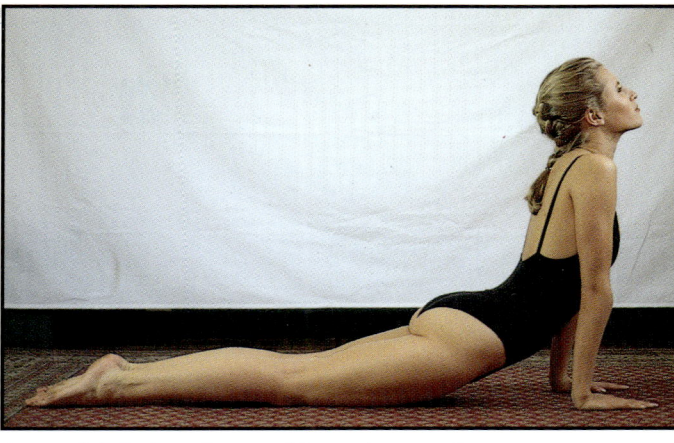

SEVEN. Inhale, lowering your hips to the ground and raising your torso. Point your toes and completely arch your back.

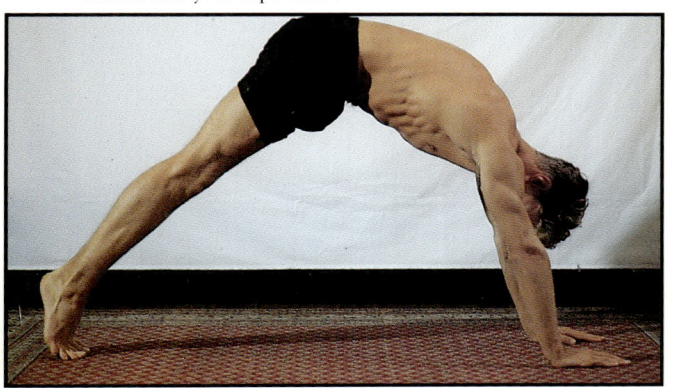

EIGHT. Exhale, raising your hips, curling your toes under and bending your head inwards. Be conscious of making a regular inverted 'V' shape.

NINE. Inhale, stepping forward with one foot between your palms. This position is the mirror image of step 4.

TWELVE. Exhale, returning to an upright position. Let your arms fall gently to your sides.

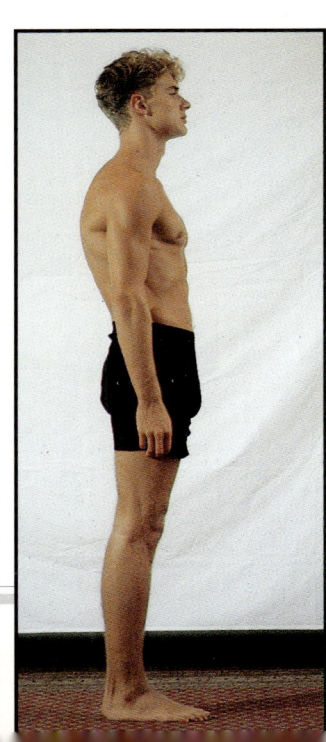

TEN. Exhale, bringing the second leg forward to join the first, as in step 3.

ELEVEN. Inhale, lifting your torso up and stretching your arms forward, then back over your head, as in step 2.

love is never lost

The end of a relationship, even an important one that you believed would last a lifetime, and in which you invested all your emotional energy, does not mean you have failed as a person.

Acknowledging that your life was going in the wrong direction is a courageous step that opens the way for positive change. Everyone needs time to work through their anger and grief after the loss of a partner, and many then embark with enthusiasm on a period of independence, but eventually the challenge of a new relationship is sure to present itself. People are resilient and adaptable. More of us are getting divorced, but there are also more remarriages than ever before, and more people living together who once were married.

The quest for love goes on, and the second time around prospective partners are wiser, more sure of their own needs and of what they can provide, and more realistic in their expectations, if no less romantic. The ability to love, once developed, is never wasted or lost. It is part of the riches that you bring to your new relationship, and which form the foundation of the future.